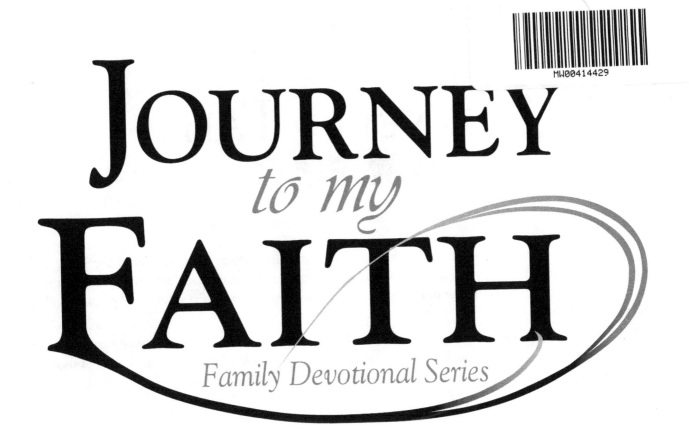

JOURNEY *to my* FAITH

Family Devotional Series

Helping Parents Develop Their Children's Love for God and for People

VOLUME 1

DAVID IBRAHIM

ANM publishers

JOURNEY to my FAITH

VOLUME 1

Paperback ISBN: 978-1-946174-04-8

Published by:

ANM
publishers

Advancing Native Missions
P.O. Box 5303
Charlottesville, VA 22905
www.AdvancingNativeMissions.com

Graphic Design by:
Christopher Kirk, GraphicsForSuccess.com

DEDICATION

Firstly, I take a great opportunity to acknowledge our Lord Jesus Christ for using this empty vessel for His glory.

Secondly, I dedicate this book to my father, who was my spiritual hero and a servant of God, Pastor James W. G. (November 29, 1927 - May 26, 2015). Also to my mother Mrs. Parveen A. G. (October 20, 1933 - April 19, 2017) a godly woman, who has a great hand in my upbringing. Both of them were godly couple, who were great inspiration to all their seven children and their spouses, as well as to their twenty one grand-children, eleven great-grand children, and also tens of thousands to whom they served passionately as their humble shepherds for over sixty years.

ACKNOWLEDGEMENT

I take this great opportunity to acknowledge and thank our Lord Jesus Christ for using this broken vessel for His glory.

As John Donne (1572–1631) said, "No man is an island…" It's amazing how, at times, the Lord puts a certain vision in our lives and brings people along the way in order to accomplish it. We, being in the "body of Christ", need one another. I don't have the words to describe my deepest gratitude, for Ms. Faye Boyd, who put in hours and hours to check the script thoroughly on each page. Ms. Boyd, thank you so much for your patience and willingness to make it possible.

I appreciate Ms. Janet Shaffer and Mr. Tommy Meche, Pastor Richard Cohen, and Annlyn Ouzts, who wholeheartedly brought the work to the next level by checking and correcting any typographical inaccuracies. Also I am grateful for Mr. Paulo R. Gill's services in research efforts, and lastly, but most importantly, for my dear wife, our children and other concerned friends, who kept encouraging and sharing new ideas to make this project possible.

Contents

INTRODUCTION

And these words which I command you today shall be in your heart. ⁷You shall teach them diligently to your children, and shall talk of them when you sit in your house, when you walk by the way, when you lie down, and when you rise up. ⁸You shall bind them as a sign on your hand, and they shall be as frontlets between your eyes." (Deuteronomy 6:6-8)

The Need

The lessons are focused and based on The Holy Bible, so that the children will learn with understanding the purpose why the Savior came for all mankind. This only could be experienced by knowing God's Word and having a personal relationship with His Son. This is the very heart of Jesus Christ that shall not perish (John 3:16).

Just as children grow physically, they also need spiritual nourishment, on a daily basis, to grow in their faith. Research has concluded that in the early stages of growth, children have the capability to absorb anything taught to them, like a sponge. This leaves a lasting impact on them for the rest of their lives.

We have seen the discipline Muslims parents have, for making sure that the children will go to the Mosque or Madrassa (Islamic school) on a daily basis. The effort behind this is to educate them with the core of Islamic faith, and for the children to memorize the whole Quran. This concept is an honor for the family, and it roots the children firm in their faith, till death. On daily basis, Muslims parents are determined to set aside one or two hours for their children to focus on their religious values and teachings.

In America or Europe, generally children attend public/government schools for 6-7 hours daily, 5 days a week, 10 months each year for the length of 12 years. Christian parents don't always have an option to implement a Christian worldview. Competing worldview is here, and subtle to imprint its on our children. Unfortunately, in our society, 90% of our children are being educated by the very system that is itself the problem. Those forces who have rejected, and have completely eliminated Biblical principals from their schools, now have embraced evolution. Therefore, this is a time of urgency. We need to be on fire for the Lord, and realize that our children are our mission field. We as Christians are not called to "fit in," but to "stand out."

Parents' Responsibility

Since the Lord has blessed us with such a wonderful gift of parenthood, we make sure to do our best to take care of children's physical needs like clothing, schooling and food. However, the question is, who is accountable to fulfill that "Spiritual Gap"? It is our responsibility to fill the void in the lives of our children, who are our Mission field. Many parents have the misconception that it's the responsibility of the "Sunday School" teachers to teach their children about Biblical values and heritage. Just 30-45 minutes a week are not enough for spiritual grooming. Rather, as parents, it's your everyday duty as Scripture commands us:

> *"This Book of the Law shall not depart from your mouth, but you shall meditate in it day and night that you may observe to do according to all that is written in it. For then you will make your way prosperous, and then you will have good success."* (Joshua 1:8)

I am humbled to share that the Lord planted a seed in my heart, to work on a daily Bible study for the families with school-aged children. The vision began when I started traveling back and forth to Pakistan. During that time duration, I met many parents who showed concern for the spiritual growth of their children. Although parents want to guide their children, they are unable to do so thoroughly and systematically, due to the lack of Biblical material that captures children's interest.

The concept of Sunday school, in third world countries, is entirely different from that in the West, where it's mostly organized according to age. However, in developing countries, due to limited space in the church building, children of all ages are accommodated in one room. The lesson is generalized from kindergarten to higher grades, therefore only major Biblical stories are taught repeatedly. The writer's desire is that this workbook will be translated into other major languages, and be circulated as an outreach tool around the world, to indigenous church groups.

Being a parent of growing children myself, this thought truly stirred my heart with a burden: that it's our responsibility to raise our children in the fear of the Lord on a daily basis at home. According to the research done and penned in the book titled *Already Gone*, by Mr. Ken Ham and his co-writers, the shocking survey result was that only 11% of the children after high school return to the church. Where are we as parents failing to do our part? Why do 89% of our children want nothing to do with Christianity anymore? This has puzzled me, and thus, after prayerfully seeking God's wisdom, the Lord gave me the vision that resulted in the birth of this workbook: *Journey to My Faith*.

Methodology

Each lesson is planned, not only to help your children, but also to help you, as a parent, learn about the basic Biblical truths. Also, much time was dedicated to gathering all the general information that makes these lessons interesting. The intention of the writer is not to overwhelm the children, although on some days you will read more than 30 Bible verses, which focus on one thought for that specific day.

End Results

The purpose of this journal is not to merely promote religious facts, but rather the Biblical and Spiritual depth of Christianity. It is a daily Bible study for the whole family, studying from Genesis through Revelation. The children will know, chronologically, the theme, purpose and synopsis of each book of the Bible, along with the number of chapters in each book. Each week, the children will memorize one or two Bible verses expressing the main foundation of our Christian faith. Also, the focus is on the

Biblical method of evangelism, which is not based on any denomination or para-church organization, but solely on the foundation of Biblical Truth. Furthermore, reading the amazing stories of great men and women of the Bible, whom God chose, will also broaden children's understanding about who the God of Abraham, Isaac and Jacob really is, and His characteristics and attributes found both in the Old and New Testaments.

Simultaneously, children will increase their general knowledge about each country, learning fascinating facts about different areas, and their global impact. They will learn about inventions, and read quotes of great men and women, who have wholeheartedly contributed to the welfare and improvement of humanity, in the fields of geography, mathematics, medicine, politics, philosophy, science, and technology. Additionally, the short weekly tests and reviews will help you evaluate what your children have studied.

As you assist your children in gaining the spiritual truths through this book, children will realize that God is more than able to use His people mightily for His glory, as long as we allow Him to work in our lives, with humility and submission. I have great confidence that one day, by God's grace, your children's names will be included in the fields of future discoveries and inventions that will benefit humanity. Primarily, though, it is important that they will be soul winners for the Lord in the years to come.

It's my humble prayer that every day, as you go through these pages with your children, the Lord will be the source of your wisdom, strength, joy, and perseverance, revealing the insights of His mysteries and revelations to you. Most importantly, I pray that whatever you do or wherever you go as a family, you will be a sweet fragrance of Christ. Others can sense the Lord's presence and reverence in your life, in all the days to come.

So I close with a quote from Solomon, which personally has touched and transformed my inner being: "The fear of the Lord is the beginning of wisdom; and the knowledge of the holy is understanding." (Proverbs 9:10)

"Your word is a lamp to my feet and a
light to my path."

Psalm 119:105

PRAYER GUIDELINES

I hope that you and your children will spend quality time in prayer, by observing Biblical principles, and by giving its ultimate importance in your daily lives.

What is Prayer?

It is communication with God, at anytime. The scriptures give some guidelines of how we are to pray. The Lord's Prayer has the complete pattern for us on how to pray…

> 5 *"And when you pray, you shall not be like the hypocrites. For they love to pray standing in the synagogues and on the corners of the streets, that they may be seen by men. Assuredly, I say to you, they have their reward.* 6 *But you, when you pray, go into your room, and when you have shut your door, pray to your Father who is in the secret place; and your Father who sees in secret will reward you openly.* 7 *And when you pray, do not use vain repetitions as the heathen do. For they think that they will be heard for their many words.* 8 *Therefore do not be like them. For your Father knows the things you have need of before you ask Him." (Matt 6:5-8)*

Ask

Although our Heavenly Father knows the things we need, we still should ask, for James tells us, *"You do not have because you do not ask."* (James 4:2-3) So it is crucial that we should keep asking, seeking and knocking. *"So I say to you, ask, and it will be given to you; seek, and you will find; knock, and it will be opened to you."* (Luke 11:9) *"Casting all your care upon Him, for He cares for you."* (1 Peter 5:7) This should comfort you as you consider the challenges and needs of you and your family. Remember that your spiritual responsibility is to daily bathe your loved ones in prayer, for their future destiny can be preserved by your prayers for them.

Intercede

The word "intercede" means, "to intervene on behalf of another." Hebrews 7:25 tells us that Jesus lives to make intercession for us. He is our Pattern, our Leader, and our Shepherd. If He is interceding for us, then we are surely called to intercede for others. Pray for those who burden your heart, or as the Holy Spirit directs you. While prayer can differ daily, intercession should be the centerpiece of prayer, not only for your family, but also for your friends, neighbors, colleagues, church, pastor, and national leaders, etc., especially for those who are nonbelievers in Jesus Christ. A very important point is that intercessory prayer takes place in the spiritual realm, where the battles are won or lost.

Speak Scriptures

During your prayer, it is very important to speak scripture verses to express that you "have faith in God." There are things we ask of God, but then He sometimes leads us to proclaim or declare things. (Mark 11:21-24) He clearly tells us that we can speak to the mountain under certain conditions and the mountains will be removed. When Satan tempts you to feel lonely, forgotten or even deserted, declare God's Word that assures you of His promise to bless and comfort you during difficult times. In order to do that, you must, *"Study to show thyself approved unto God."* (2 Tim. 2:15)

In your prayers speak God's Word over you, your family members, and friends. Remember those scriptural assurances that *"by His stripes, we are healed"* (Isaiah 53:5), *"All my needs are met according to His riches in glory by Christ Jesus"* (Philippians 4:19), and, most importantly, *"I can do all things through Christ who strengthens me"* (Philippians 4:13).

Repentance

Many of us understand the term "repentance" means "turning from sin." However, the biblical definition of "repent" means "to change one's mind." The Bible also tells us that true repentance will result in a change of actions (Luke 3:8-14; Acts 3:19). So, the full biblical definition of repentance is, a change of mind that results in a change of action. Acts 26:20 declares, *"I preached that they should repent and turn to God and prove their repentance by their deeds. For godly sorrow produces repentance leading to salvation, not to be regretted; but the sorrow of the world produces death."* (2 Corinthians 7:10)

The Lord tells us in Psalm 51:17 that He will not turn away a broken and contrite or repentant heart! He will not turn us away! God's Word clearly says that, if one hides iniquity in his heart, He will not hear him. (Psalm 66:18) So once you give Him thanks, praise and worship, your heart is open to confess your sins. When you've done this, you need to believe by faith that your sins truly are forgiven, and the result will be great inner peace. He not only forgives your sins, He will also enable you to resist leaning toward rebellion and independence, if you ask.

Enjoy His Presence

As you spend great quality time with Jesus, render unto Him praise and thanksgiving, and speak the Word, you will sense Him very near and will enjoy His presence.

During your prayer time, worship, read, meditate, and rejoice in a God who hears you when you call on His name. The scripture clearly assures us through the Words spoken to Jeremiah, *"For I know the thoughts that I think toward you, says the Lord, thoughts of peace and not of evil, to give you a future and a hope. [12] Then you will call upon Me and go and pray to Me, and I will listen to you. [13] And you will seek Me and find Me, when you search for Me with all your heart."* (Jeremiah 29.11-13)

While or when you focusing on God's provisions, mercies, and goodness He has brought into your life. He will fill you with the joy of His presence. Always have an attitude of praise and thanksgiving in whatever circumstances you experience, so that His grace will sustain you, and to make you victorious through His Cross. It's very important that your opening and closing prayer each day of the study be done with humility and openness of heart, thus this will render your prayer meaningful and genuine.

"The Lord bless you, and keep you: the Lord make his face to shine upon you, and be gracious unto you; The Lord lift up his countenance upon you, and give you peace." (Numbers 6:24)

Day 1 ~ The Beginning

OPENING PRAYER

READ: Genesis 1:1-2; Exodus 20:11; Psalm 33:6-9; John 1:1-5; Colossians 1:16 & Revelation 4:11

In the Beginning...

1) What is the Biblical creation?—————————————————————

——

2) Who created the earth and heavens?————————————————————

——

3) How did the universe come into existence?————————————————

——

Explore God's World

MEMORY VERSES:

Genesis 1:27 "So God created humankind in His image, in the image of God He created them; male and female He created them."

Psalm 33:6 "By the word of the Lord the heavens were made, and all the host of them by the breath of His mouth."

GENESIS	THEME
1st book of the Bible with 50 chapters	The blessed beginning

For Your Information

FUN FACTS	THE WORLD CONTINENTS	AFGHANISTAN
1. The color blue is the least common color in the natural foods we eat. 2. The kite, invented roughly 2,500 to 3,000 years ago, originated in China, Malaysia or Indonesia.	Asia, Africa, Australia, Antarctica, Europe, North America, and South America. (Some scholars refer to Asia and Europe as Eurasia while North and South America as Americas)	…is in the continent of Asia; Kabul is the capital. The name comes from the Persian word meaning "Land of the Afghans." Afghanistan is a landlocked mountainous country bordered by Pakistan, Iran, Turkmenistan, Uzbekistan, Tajikistan, and China. The country is known for producing some of the finest pomegranates, grapes, apricots, melons, and several other fresh and dry fruits, including nuts.

GROUP DISCUSSION AND CLOSING PRAYER

"What you are is God's gift to you; what you become is your gift to God."

Hans Urs von Balthasar, Prayer

Day 2 ~ The First Six Days

OPENING PRAYER
READ: Genesis 1:3-30

And God said...

1) Describe what God did each day_____

_____

_____

2) Why did God create man on the last day?_____

_____

3) When God created Adam, why did God say, "It's very good"? _____

_____

Explore God's World

MEMORY VERSES:

Genesis 1:27 "So God created humankind in His image, in the image of God He created them; male and female He created them."

Psalm 33:6 "By the word of the Lord the heavens were made, and all the host of them by the breath of His mouth."

EXODUS	THEME
2nd book of the Bible with 40 chapters	The redemption of the covenant nation

For Your Information

FUN FACTS	THE WORLD CONTINENTS	ALBANIA
1. Putting sugar directly on a wound or cut can help with the healing process. 2. Lego is a very popular interlocking plastic toy. The LEGO toy company was founded by Ole Kirk Christiansen of Denmark in 1932.	Asia, Africa, Australia, Antarctica, Europe, North America, and South America. (Some scholars refer to Asia and Europe as Eurasia while North and South America as Americas)	...is in the continent of Europe; Tirana is the capital. The golden eagle is the national symbol. Albania produces significant amounts of wheat, corn, tobacco, and figs. Football (soccer) is the most popular sport. Mother Teresa was Albanian.

GROUP DISCUSSION AND CLOSING PRAYER

"He is no fool who gives what he cannot keep, to gain what he cannot lose."

Jim Elliot, Christian Missionary

Day 3 ~ Adam & Eve

OPENING PRAYER
READ: Genesis 2:1-25

Thus the heavens...

1) What is the importance of the seventh day in our lives? _____
_____
_____

2) Who were the first man and woman? What were their characteristics? _____
_____

3) What responsibility and authority were given to Adam and Eve? _____
_____

Explore God's World

MEMORY VERSES:
Genesis 1:27 "So God created humankind in His image, in the image of God He created them; male and female He created them."
Psalm 33:6 "By the word of the Lord the heavens were made, and all the host of them by the breath of His mouth."

LEVITICUS	THEME
3rd book of the Bible with 27 chapters	Holiness

For Your Information

FUN FACTS	THE WORLD CONTINENTS	ALGERIA
1. Ernest V. Wright wrote a 50,000 word book titled Gadsby in which he did not use the letter 'e'. 2. In 1609 Galileo was the first to use a telescope for the purpose of astronomy. He is commonly credited for inventing the telescope.	Asia, Africa, Australia, Antarctica, Europe, North America, and South America. (Some scholars refer to Asia and Europe as Eurasia while North and South America as Americas)	...is in the continent of Africa; Algiers is the capital. Algeria is the largest country in Africa and the Arab world. Their road network is the most densest of the African continent. Service in the military is compulsory for men aged 19-30 for 18 months.

GROUP DISCUSSION AND CLOSING PRAYER

"Worry does not empty tomorrow of its sorrows; it empties today of its strength."
Corrie Ten Boom, Protector of Jewish People during the Holocaust

Day 4 ~ The Fall

Now the serpent...

1) What did the serpent say to the woman? _____

_____

_____

2) Why did Adam and Eve hide themselves from God? _____

_____

3) What were the punishments for Eve, Adam and the serpent? _____

_____

Explore God's World

MEMORY VERSES:

Genesis 1:27 "So God created humankind in His image, in the image of God He created them; male and female He created them."

Psalm 33:6 "By the word of the Lord the heavens were made, and all the host of them by the breath of His mouth."

NUMBERS	THEME
4th book of the Bible with 36 chapters	Purging Israel for entry into the promised land

For Your Information

FUN FACTS	THE WORLD CONTINENTS	ANDORRA
1. Garrett Augustus Morgan (1877-1963) invented a traffic signal and developed the gas mask. 2. Richard G. Drew (1899-1980) invented masking tape and clear adhesive tape. Drew was an engineer for the 3M company (the Minnesota Mining and Manufacturing Company).	Asia, Africa, Australia, Antarctica, Europe, North America, and South America. (Some scholars refer to Asia and Europe as Eurasia while North and South America as Americas)	...is in the continent of Europe; Andorra La Vella is capital. The official language is Catalan, although Spanish, Portuguese, and French are also commonly spoken. Children between the ages of 6 & 16 are required by law to have full-time education.

GROUP DISCUSSION AND CLOSING PRAYER

"God is most glorified in us when we are most satisfied in Him."

John Piper

Day 5 ~ Abel & Cain

Now Adam knew...

1) Who was the older brother? Whose sacrifice was accepted and why? _____

_____

_____

2) What is important, our sacrifice or our attitude? _____

_____

3) What was the cause of Abel's death? _____

_____

Explore God's World

MEMORY VERSES:
Genesis 1:27 "So God created humankind in His image, in the image of God He created them;
   male and female He created them."
Psalm 33:6 "By the word of the Lord the heavens were made, and all the host of them by the
   breath of His mouth."

DEUTERONOMY	THEME
5th book of the Bible with 36 chapters	Moses' sermons on the law

For Your Information

FUN FACTS	THE WORLD CONTINENTS	ANGOLA
1. Blood centers often run short of types O and B red blood cells. 2. There is enough concrete in the Hoover Dam to pave a two lane highway from San Francisco to New York.	Asia, Africa, Australia, Antarctica, Europe, North America, and South America. (Some scholars refer to Asia and Europe as Eurasia while North and South America as Americas)	...is in the continent of Africa; Luanda is the capital. The name comes from the Portuguese colony of Reino de Angola (Kingdom of Angola). Through the Atlantic slave trade, Angola provided a large number of black slaves to merchants and slave dealers.

GROUP DISCUSSION AND CLOSING PRAYER

"To know is to know that you know nothing. That is the meaning of true knowledge."

Socrates

Day 6 ~ The Sin

OPENING PRAYER

READ: Deuteronomy 25:16; Proverbs 6:16-19; Isaiah 59:2, 64:6; Romans 3:10-12, 23; 5:12; and 1st John 3:4

As it is written...

1) What is sin and its consequences? _____

_____

2) What is the 7th sin? _____

_____

3) How can you overcome sin? Who paid the price for your sins? _____

_____

4) What is the main cause of sin? _____

_____

Explore God's World

MEMORY VERSES:

Genesis 1:27 "So God created humankind in His image, in the image of God He created them; male and female He created them."

Psalm 33:6 "By the word of the Lord the heavens were made, and all the host of them by the breath of His mouth."

JOSHUA	THEME
6th book of the Bible with 24 chapters	The strenuous task of taking possession of God's gifts

For Your Information

FUN FACTS	THE WORLD CONTINENTS	ANTIGUA AND BARBUDA
1. Of all 5 senses, your sense of hearing becomes less sharp after you eat too much. 2. An acre of trees can remove about 13 tons of dust and gases every year from the surrounding environment.	Asia, Africa, Australia, Antarctica, Europe, North America, and South America. (Some scholars refer to Asia and Europe as Eurasia while North and South America as Americas)	...is in the continent of South America; Saint John's is the capital. The country is nicknamed "Land of 365 Beaches." Its governance, language, and culture have all been strongly influenced by the British Empire. The famous Cricketer Sir Vivian Richards is from here.

GROUP DISCUSSION AND CLOSING PRAYER

"The best and most beautiful things in the world cannot be seen or even touched-they must be felt with the heart."

Helen Keller

Day 7 ~ Week in Review

COMPLETE THE FOLLOWING

a. After completing His creation God said, _____

b. The joy of living in God's perfect garden was_____

c. Cain reacted to God's correction by_____

d. The serpent said to the woman _____

e. Mother Teresa was_____

f. The 4th book of the Bible is _____; it has _____chapters

g. The famous Cricketer Sir Vivian Richards is from_____

h. The name_____ comes from the Portuguese colony of Reino de Angola.

i. _____is the largest country in Africa and the Arab world.

MEMORIZE AND WRITE

Genesis 1:27_____

_____

_____

Psalm 33:6_____

_____

_____

TRUE OR FALSE — Circle T for true or F for false

T or F   Tirana is the capital of Afghanistan.

T or F   The first thing which God created was Adam.

T or F   There are presently nine continents, which are inhabited.

T or F   The theme of Numbers is "Moses' Sermons on the Law."

T or F   Leviticus is the 3rd book of the Bible and has 27 chapters.

T or F   Afghanistan requires full-time education for children ages 6 to 16.

T or F   The famous Cricketer Sir Vivian Richards is from Angola.

MATCH THE FOLLOWING

_____ a. Genesis

_____ b. Numbers

_____ c. Leviticus

_____ d. Exodus

_____ e. Antigua and Barbuda

_____ f. Algeria

_____ g. Afghanistan

_____ h. Joshua

_____ i. Albania

_____ j. Angola

_____ k. Deuteronomy

_____ l. Andorra

1. Algiers

2. Andorra La Vella

3. Saint John

4. Purging Israel for entry into the promised land

5. The Blessed Beginning

6. Luanda

7. Mother Teresa

8. Moses' Sermons on the Law

9. 6th book of the Bible and has 24 chapters.

10. Kabul

11. The Redemption of the Covenant Nation

12. Holiness

LIST THE SEVEN CONTINENTS

1. _____

2. _____

3. _____

4. _____

5. _____

6. _____

7. _____

Day 8 ~ The Living Word

OPENING PRAYER
READ: Joshua 1:8;
Psalm 119:5; John 1:1;
Romans 15:4; and
2nd Timothy 3:16-17

All Scripture is given...

1) What does the Holy Bible mean to you? _____
_____
_____

2) Explain, "Your word is a lamp for my feet, a light on my path"? _____
_____

3) What is the message of the Bible and who speaks to you through the Bible? _____
_____

Explore God's World

MEMORY VERSES:

Joshua 1:8 "This Book of the Law shall not depart from your mouth, but you shall meditate in it day and night, that you may observe to do according to all that is written in it. For then you will make your way prosperous, and then you will have good success."

JUDGES	THEME
7th book of the Bible with 21 chapters	Cycle of decline and renewal among God's people

For Your Information

FUN FACTS	THE TEN LARGEST COUNTRIES BY LAND MASS	ARGENTINA
1. In 1967, the 1st successful heart transplant was performed in Cape Town, South Africa. 2. Joseph Gayetty invented toilet paper in 1857. His new toilet paper was composed of flat sheets. Before his invention, people tore pages out of mail order catalogs.	1) Russia 2) Canada 3) China 4) USA 5) Brazil 6) Australia 7) India 8) Argentina 9) Kazakhstan 10) Algeria	...is in the continent of South America; Buenos Aires is the capital. The country's name is derived from Latin "argentum" ("silver", "plata"). Argentina is the 8th largest country in the world with the total area (1,073,518 sq miles), the 2nd largest in Latin America, and the largest Spanish-speaking nation.

GROUP DISCUSSION AND CLOSING PRAYER

"Don't judge each day by the harvest you reap, but by the seeds that you plant."

Robert Louis Stevenson

Day 9 ~ Brief History & Authenticity of the Bible

Who through Him...

OPENING PRAYER

READ: Genesis 1:1-2; Psalm 33:4; 2nd Timothy 3:16-17; and Revelation 22:18-19

The English word "Bible" comes from bíblia (Latin) and bíblos in (Greek). The term means "book" or "books" and may have originated from the ancient Egyptian port of Byblos (in modern-day Lebanon) where papyrus (used for making books and scrolls) was exported to Greece.

The Bible is a compilation of 66 books and letters written by more than 40 authors during a period of approximately 1,500 years. The authors of the Bible are from diverse backgrounds and countries. These authors included, among others, Moses, an official in Egypt; Amos, a farmer; Daniel, a minister in Babylon; Jeremiah and Ezekiel, priests; Peter and John, fishermen; Matthew, a tax collector; Luke, a physician; and Paul, a Pharisee.

The Old Testament was written for the most part in Hebrew, with a small percentage in Aramaic. The New Testament was written in Koine [common or everyday language] Greek. (http://christianity.about.com/od/glossary/qt/Bible-Definition.htm)

1) What does "Bible" mean?_____

2) The Old and New Testaments were written in what languages? _____

_____

3) How many Authors wrote the Bible? The Bible was written over a period of how many years?

_____

Explore God's World

MEMORY VERSES:

Joshua 1:8 "This Book of the Law shall not depart from your mouth, but you shall meditate in it day and night, that you may observe to do according to all that is written in it. For then you will make your way prosperous, and then you will have good success."

RUTH	**THEME**
8th book of the Bible with 4 chapters	Relative-Redemption

For Your Information

FUN FACTS	**THE TEN LARGEST COUNTRIES BY LAND MASS**	**ARMENIA**
1. Ostriches can run faster than horses, and the males can roar like lions. 2. In Germany, publicly denying the Holocaust earns a prison sentence.	1) Russia 2) Canada 3) China 4) USA 5) Brazil 6) Australia 7) India 8) Argentina 9) Kazakhstan 10) Algeria	...is in the continent of Asia; Yerevan is the capital. The people have their own unique alphabet, which was invented by Mesrop Mashtots in 405 AD. Armenia lies in the Mountains of Ararat, upon which Noah's Ark came to rest after the flood. (Gen.8:4).

GROUP DISCUSSION AND CLOSING PRAYER

"Nothing is impossible. The word itself says 'I'm possible'!"

Audrey Hepburn

Day 10 ~ Reaching the Unreached

And this gospel...

OPENING PRAYER

READ: Matthew 24:14; Romans 11:25; and Revelation 14:6-7

United Bible Societies (UBS) have claimed that at least part of the Bible has been translated into more than 2,530 languages. This includes the whole Old or New Testaments in 1,715 languages, plus 55 sign languages. As of December of 2011, UBS had the complete text of the Bible in 475 languages. (http://www.unitedbiblesocieties.org/news/1525-full-bible-now-available-in-475-languages)

According to Wycliffe Bible translators, 2,789 people groups have access to at least a book of the Bible, including 1,005 languages groups with a book or more; 1,275 language groups have access to the New Testament in their native languages. As of September, 2012, 518 language groups have the complete Bible. It is estimated by Wycliffe Bible translators that there are 1,967 languages (representing around 200 million people) that have yet to have any form of Bible translation. They also estimate 2,000 languages projects are currently in process. (Wycliffe Bible Translators; What's been done, what's left to do. access date=2013-01-21, "Translation, Literacy and Language Statistics." Wycliffe.org)

Explore God's World

MEMORY VERSES:

Joshua 1:8 "This Book of the Law shall not depart from your mouth, but you shall meditate in it day and night, that you may observe to do according to all that is written in it. For then you will make your way prosperous, and then you will have good success."

1ST SAMUEL	THEME
9th book of the Bible with 31 chapters	From theocracy to monarchy

For Your Information

FUN FACTS	THE TEN LARGEST COUNTRIES BY LAND MASS	ARUBA
1. Bill Gates' house was partially designed by the Macintosh computer. 2. The color orange was named after the fruit and not the other way around.	1) Russia 2) Canada 3) China 4) USA 5) Brazil 6) Australia 7) India 8) Argentina 9) Kazakhstan 10) Algeria	...is in the continent of North America; Oranjestad is the capital. Dutch is the official language, but since 2003, Papiamento is the predominant language. Aruba, which is only 20 km long, has five main industries: tourism, gold and phosphate mining, aloe and petroleum refining. The country is only 20 miles (33 km) long.

GROUP DISCUSSION AND CLOSING PRAYER

"God always gives His best to those who leave the choice with him."

Jim Elliot

Day 11 ~ Old & New Testament

OPENING PRAYER

READ: Matthew 26:28-29; and Hebrews 9:16-17, 22

For there is a testament...

Testament is simply a document that the author has sworn to be true. From the Biblical perspective, it is a covenant (testament) between God and humans. Knowing the difference between the Old and New Testaments is one of the most important foundations to properly understand God's Word. There is a total of sixty six (66) books in the both Old and New Testaments.

1) What does "testament" (covenant) mean to you? _____

_____

_____

2) What is the importance of the testament (covenant) in your life? _____

_____

3) Who has the responsibility to share the Old & New Testament with others? _____

_____

Explore God's World

MEMORY VERSES:

Joshua 1:8 "This Book of the Law shall not depart from your mouth, but you shall meditate in it day and night, that you may observe to do according to all that is written in it. For then you will make your way prosperous, and then you will have good success."

2ND SAMUEL	THEME
10th book of the Bible with 24 chapters	The establishment of David's kingdom

For Your Information

FUN FACTS	THE TEN LARGEST COUNTRIES BY LAND MASS	AUSTRALIA
1. Jesse W. Reno was an American inventor who developed the first escalator in 1891. 2. Jonas Salk formulated a vaccine against the devastating disease polio, also called Infantile (childish) paralysis.	1) Russia 2) Canada 3) China 4) USA 5) Brazil 6) Australia 7) India 8) Argentina 9) Kazakhstan 10) Algeria	...is the mainland of the Australian continent; Canberra is the capital. The country includes the island of Tasmania and numerous smaller islands. Australia is also known as Aussie and it's the world's 6th largest country by total area. Australia was inhabited by the "first peoples or indigenous Aborigines," among whom there are roughly 250 language groups.

GROUP DISCUSSION AND CLOSING PRAYER

"Nothing is impossible. The word itself says 'I'm possible'!"

Audrey Hepburn

Day 12 ~ The Old Testament Has 39 Books
...which are divided into five categories

The Torah or Law
> Genesis, Exodus, Leviticus, Numbers, Deuteronomy

The Historical Books
> Joshua Judges, Ruth, 1st Samuel, 2nd Samuel, 1st Kings, 2nd Kings, 1st Chronicles, 2nd Chronicles, Ezra, Nehemiah, Esther

Poetry & Wisdom
> Job, Psalms, Proverbs, Ecclesiastes, Song of Solomon

The Major Prophets
> Isaiah, Jeremiah, Lamentations, Ezekiel, Daniel

The Twelve Minor Prophets
> Hosea, Joel, Amos, Obadiah, Jonah, Micah, Nahum, Habakkuk, Zephaniah, Haggai, Zechariah, and Malachi

1) Into how many sections is the Old Testament divided? _____

2) Which books are in the Torah and Poetry? _____

_____

3) Ezra, Malachi, Daniel, Esther, Joel, Isaiah, Haggai, and Job are part of which sections?

_____

Explore God's World
MEMORY VERSES:

Joshua 1:8 "This Book of the Law shall not depart from your mouth, but you shall meditate in it day and night, that you may observe to do according to all that is written in it. For then you will make your way prosperous, and then you will have good success."

1ST KINGS 11th book of the Bible with 22 chapters	**THEME** From glorious unity to idolatrous division

For Your Information

FUN FACTS	**THE TEN LARGEST COUNTRIES BY LAND MASS**	**AUSTRIA**
1. If you Google "Zerg rush" Google will eat up the search engine. 2. Samuel Finley Breese Morse (1791-1872), inventor and painter, built the first American telegraph around 1835. (It was also being developed independently in Europe).	1) Russia 2) Canada 3) China 4) USA 5) Brazil 6) Australia 7) India 8) Argentina 9) Kazakhstan 10) Algeria	...is in the continent of Europe; Vienna is the capital. The German name for Austria, Österreich, means "eastern kingdom" or "eastern empire." Austria is the 12th richest country in the world (GDP). The famous music composer Mozart was Austrian.

GROUP DISCUSSION AND CLOSING PRAYER
"We can't help everyone, but everyone can help someone."
Ronald Reagan

Day 13 ~ The New Testament Has 27 Books
...which are divided into five categories

Gospels
 Matthew, Mark, Luke, and John
History
 Acts
Letters of Paul
 Romans, 1st Corinthians, 2nd Corinthians, Galatians, Ephesians, Philippians, Colossians, 1st
 Thessalonians, 2nd Thessalonians, 1st Timothy, 2nd Timothy, Titus, Philemon
General Letters
 Hebrews [perhaps by Paul], James, 1st Peter, 2nd Peter, 1st John, 2nd John, 3rd John, Jude
Prophecy
 Revelation

1) What are the different divisions of the New Testament? _____

2) Which books are gospel, history and prophecy? _____

_____

3) Name those Letters which are written by Apostle Paul. _____

_____

Explore God's World

MEMORY VERSES:

Joshua 1:8 "This Book of the Law shall not depart from your mouth, but you shall meditate in it day and night, that you may observe to do according to all that is written in it. For then you will make your way prosperous, and then you will have good success."

2ND KINGS	**THEME**
12th book of the Bible with 25 chapters	The plunge into disciplinary exile

For Your Information

FUN FACTS	THE TEN LARGEST COUNTRIES BY LAND MASS	AZERBAIJAN
1. The idea to divide the Earth into time zones was proposed by Sir Sandford Fleming. 2. The average high school student today has the same level of anxiety as the average psychiatric patient in the early 1950's.	1) Russia 2) Canada 3) China 4) USA 5) Brazil 6) Australia 7) India 8) Argentina 9) Kazakhstan 10) Algeria	...is in the continent of Asia; Baku is the capital. Nearly half of all the mud volcanoes on earth can be found in Azerbaijan. The country borders Armenia, Iran, Georgia, Russia and Turkey. Two-thirds of the land is rich in oil and natural gas.

GROUP DISCUSSION AND CLOSING PRAYER

"Whoever is happy will make others happy too."
Anne Frank

Day 14 ~ Week in Review

TRUE OR FALSE — Circle T for true or F for false

T or F   Job and Psalms are historical books.

T or F   Nassau is the capital of the Bahamas.

T or F   Matthew, Mark, Luke, and John are the gospels.

T or F   Testament simply means covenant.

T or F   1st Kings is the 5th book of the Bible.

T or F   Jonah, Micah, and Nahum are minor prophets.

T or F   The nation of Austria is in the continent of Australia.

T or F   Ruth is the 8th book of the Bible and has 4 chapters.

T or F   America and Canada are the smallest countries land wise.

T or F   The Bible is a compilation of 66 books.

MEMORIZE AND WRITE

Joshua 1:8 _____

_____

_____

CIRCLE THE CORRECT ANSWER

a. Do you think that the Bible is the true Word of God?

    1) Yes   2) No   3) Not Sure

b. Old and New Testament are the covenant between man and God?

    1) Yes   2) No   3) Not Sure

c. Is it important to spread the message of Gospel to the whole world?

    1) Yes   2) No   3) Not Sure

d. Does the Old Testament lead to Jesus Christ?

    1) Yes   2) No   3) Not Sure

e. The Old Testament is about the laws of God and the New Testament is all about grace?

    1) Yes   2) No   3) Not Sure

SUMMARIZE, IN A FEW WORDS, THE NECESSITY OF THE HOLY BIBLE.

_____

_____

_____

WHY IS IT IMPORTANT TO KNOW THE HISTORY OF THE BIBLE?

_____

_____

_____

LIST THE TEN LARGEST COUNTRIES BY LAND MASS.

_____

_____

_____

Bible Word Search

```
C A N M E A E J M B G S P H U
B H K O U L E Z E W U T R A P
P R R H M R I R R S S N O C A
E V S I E O E J E A O V V I U
E O L M S A L J A I F B E M L
J F I G N T K O T H Z G R A W
D A N I E L I C S P F J B M E
H B G D O W E A R U T H S G H
D G C U E R X K N N E O R E T
G I I Q R O Y S I S E N E G T
F X V U T M B S E S O M Q N A
K Z S A M A L K W O I S G M M
J E O D D N V X R X L I S C G
R C D W Y S B F C I B E N L U
W R E V E L A T I O N D O T M
```

BEREAN	CHRISTIAN	DANIEL
DAVID	ELIJAH	EZRA
GENESIS	JEREMIAH	JESUS
JOSHUA	MATTHEW	MICAH
MOSES	PAUL	PROVERBS
RESURRECTION	REVELATION	ROMANS
RUTH	SOLOMON	

Day 15 ~ Noah

OPENING PRAYER

READ: Genesis 5:32; 6:1-10; and 9:20-23

And Noah was five hundred years old...

1) Why was God not happy with the human race during Noah's day? _____
_____
_____

2) What were the names of Noah's sons? _____
_____

3) What was Noah's sin as recorded in the Bible? _____
_____

Explore God's World

MEMORY VERSES:

Deuteronomy 6:7-8 "You shall teach them diligently to your children, and shall talk of them when you sit in your house, when you walk by the way, when you lie down, and when you rise up. You shall bind them as a sign on your hand, and they shall be as frontlets between your eyes."

1ST CHRONICLES	THEME
13th book of the Bible with 29 chapters	David, the man after God's own heart

For Your Information

FUN FACTS	THE TEN LARGEST COUNTRIES BY POPULATION	THE BAHAMAS
1. New Jersey is home to the world's 1st drive-in movie theater. 2. Sweat itself is odorless. It's the bacteria on the skin that mingles with sweat to produce body odor.	1) China 2) India 3) United States of America 4) Indonesia 5) Brazil 6) Pakistan 7) Nigeria 8) Bangladesh 9) Russia 10) Japan	...is in the continent of North America; Nassau is the capital. The country is one of only two countries whose official name begins with the word "the", while The Gambia is the other country. There are over 700 islands and cays. The national Sport is sloop sailing.

GROUP DISCUSSION AND CLOSING PRAYER

"Be faithful to that which exists within yourself."

Andre Gide

Day 16 ~ Noah & the Ark

OPENING PRAYER
READ: Genesis 6:11-22

The earth also was corrupt...

1) What did God say to Noah about the people on earth? _____

_____

_____

2) What were the measurements of the ark? _____

_____

3) How long did it take Noah to build the ark? _____

_____

Explore God's World

MEMORY VERSES:

Deuteronomy 6:7-8 "You shall teach them diligently to your children, and shall talk of them when you sit in your house, when you walk by the way, when you lie down, and when you rise up. You shall bind them as a sign on your hand, and they shall be as frontlets between your eyes."

2ND CHRONICLES	THEME
14th book of the Bible with 26 chapters	The glory of Solomon and the decay of Judah

For Your Information

FUN FACTS	THE TEN LARGEST COUNTRIES BY POPULATION	BAHRAIN
1. Vatican City is not a member of the United Nations. 2. Found in the Pacific Ocean, the Mariana Trench is the deepest known point in the world's oceans.	1) China 2) India 3) United States of America 4) Indonesia 5) Brazil 6) Pakistan 7) Nigeria 8) Bangladesh 9) Russia 10) Japan	...is in the continent of Asia; Manama is the capital. Bahrain is also known as the Kingdom of Bahrain. Houda Nonoo was appointed ambassador to the US from 2008 to 2013, making her the first Jewish ambassador of any Arab country. In 2011, Alice Samaan, a Christian woman, was appointed ambassador to the United Kingdom.

GROUP DISCUSSION AND CLOSING PRAYER

"There are two ways of spreading light: to be the candle or the mirror that reflects it."

Edith Wharton

Day 17 ~ Noah & the Great Flood

OPENING PRAYER
READ: Genesis 7:1-24

Then the Lord said to Noah...

1) What kind people did God allow into the ark? _____

_____

_____

2) What types and numbers of clean and unclean animals entered in the ark? _____

_____

3) For how many days or months did Noah remain in the ark? _____

_____

Explore God's World

MEMORY VERSES:

Deuteronomy 6:7-8 "You shall teach them diligently to your children, and shall talk of them when you sit in your house, when you walk by the way, when you lie down, and when you rise up. You shall bind them as a sign on your hand, and they shall be as frontlets between your eyes."

EZRA	THEME
15th book of the Bible with 10 chapters	Return to restore worship and morality

For Your Information

FUN FACTS	THE TEN LARGEST COUNTRIES BY POPULATION	BANGLADESH
1. The Chinese used fingerprints as a method of identification as far back as 700 AD.	1) China 2) India	...is in the continent of Asia; Dhaka is the capital. Before 1971 the country was known as East Pakistan. Muhammad Yunus (awarded the Nobel Peace Prize) was a significant contributor to the development of the economy by means of microcredit.
2. In Japan, 90% of cell phones are waterproof because youngsters use them even in the shower.	3) United States of America 4) Indonesia 5) Brazil 6) Pakistan 7) Nigeria 8) Bangladesh 9) Russia 10) Japan	

GROUP DISCUSSION AND CLOSING PRAYER

"Look, don't judge Christianity by the imperfect examples that we have seen in history. Judge it by Jesus Christ."

Chuck Smith

Day 18 ~ Noah Deliverance

OPENING PRAYER
READ: Genesis 8:1-22

The earth also was corrupt...

1) How was the whole earth flooded? _____
_____
_____

2) At what month did the waters start to decrease? _____
_____

3) What was the covenant between God and Creation? _____
_____

Explore God's World

MEMORY VERSES:

Deuteronomy 6:7-8 "You shall teach them diligently to your children, and shall talk of them when you sit in your house, when you walk by the way, when you lie down, and when you rise up. You shall bind them as a sign on your hand, and they shall be as frontlets between your eyes."

NEHEMIAH	THEME
16th book of the Bible with 13 chapters	Revitalizing a nation

For Your Information

FUN FACTS	THE TEN LARGEST COUNTRIES BY POPULATION	BARBADOS
1. Donald Duck's full name is Donald Fauntleroy Duck. 2. Vampire bats are one of the few mammals known to adopt orphans, and to share food with less fortunate roost mates.	1) China 2) India 3) United States of America 4) Indonesia 5) Brazil 6) Pakistan 7) Nigeria 8) Bangladesh 9) Russia 10) Japan	...is in the continent of North America; Bridgetown is the capital. English is the official language. Barbados' literacy rate, which ranks in the top 5 countries, is close to 100%. Camouflage clothing is reserved for military use. Thus, it's forbidden for civilians and children to wear.

GROUP DISCUSSION AND CLOSING PRAYER

"I don't need a successor, only willing hands to accept the torch for a new generation."

Billy Graham

Day 19 ~ Noah God's Covenant

OPENING PRAYER
READ: Genesis 9:1-17

So God blessed Noah and his sons...

1) What do we find in verses 1 and 7? _____
_____
_____

2) What does God allow Noah and his sons to eat? _____
_____

3) What does the rainbow represent? _____
_____

Explore God's World

MEMORY VERSES:

Deuteronomy 6:7-8 "You shall teach them diligently to your children, and shall talk of them when you sit in your house, when you walk by the way, when you lie down, and when you rise up. You shall bind them as a sign on your hand, and they shall be as frontlets between your eyes."

ESTHER	THEME
17th book of the Bible with 10 chapters	God's Sovereign Protection of His Chosen People

For Your Information

FUN FACTS	THE TEN LARGEST COUNTRIES BY POPULATION	BELARUS
1. "Dimension 6" was the original name for "Nike". 2. Real diamonds have a radiolucent molecular structure, which means that they don't appear in x-ray images.	1) China 2) India 3) United States of America 4) Indonesia 5) Brazil 6) Pakistan 7) Nigeria 8) Bangladesh 9) Russia 10) Japan	...is in the continent of Europe; Minsk is the capital. Famous for its opera and ballet, Belarus borders the countries of Latvia, Lithuania, Poland, Russia, and Ukraine. Most of the economy remains state-controlled and is described as "Soviet-style."

GROUP DISCUSSION AND CLOSING PRAYER

"I would rather have the wrong facts and a right attitude, than right facts and a wrong attitude"

Chuck Smith

Day 20 ~ Noah & His Sons' Blessings

OPENING PRAYER
READ: Genesis 9:1-17

Now the sons...

1) What was the cause of Noah's nakedness? _____
_____

2) What did Ham tell his brothers? _____
_____

3) Which son was cursed and who received the blessings? _____
_____

4) After the flood, how many years did Noah live? How old was Noah when he died? _____
_____

Explore God's World

MEMORY VERSES:

Deuteronomy 6:7-8 "You shall teach them diligently to your children, and shall talk of them when you sit in your house, when you walk by the way, when you lie down, and when you rise up. You shall bind them as a sign on your hand, and they shall be as frontlets between your eyes."

JOB	THEME
18th book of the Bible with 42 chapters	The sovereignty of God in human suffering

For Your Information

FUN FACTS	THE TEN LARGEST COUNTRIES BY POPULATION	BELGIUM
1. "Phonophobia" is the fear of loud sounds, voices or of one's own voice. 2. Radar is short for Radio Detection And Ranging. The first practical radar system was invented in 1935 by Sir Robert Alexander Watson-Watt.	1) China 2) India 3) United States of America 4) Indonesia 5) Brazil 6) Pakistan 7) Nigeria 8) Bangladesh 9) Russia 10) Japan	...is in the continent of Europe; Brussels is the capital. Belgium's main exports are machinery, equipment, chemicals, and finished diamonds. The three official languages are Dutch, French and German. The saxophone was invented in1840's by Adolphe Sax.

GROUP DISCUSSION AND CLOSING PRAYER

"The strongest of all warriors are these two-Time and Patience."

Leo Tolstoy

Day 21 ~ Week in Review

READ AND EXPLAIN IN YOUR OWN WORDS

a. Genesis 6:6 _____

_____

b. Genesis 6:9 "Noah walked with God" _____

_____

c. Genesis 8:21 "The Lord said in His heart" _____

_____

d. Genesis 9:1 "Be fruitful and multiply, and fill the earth" _____

_____

e. Genesis 9:9 "And as for Me, behold, I establish My covenant" ____

_____

TRUE OR FALSE — Circle T for true or F for false

T or F   Ezra is the 13th book of the Bible with 29 chapters.

T or F   David is known as the man after God's own heart.

T or F   The Bahamas' national sport is sloop sailing.

T or F   Alice Samaan, a Christian woman was appointed ambassador to the UK.

T or F   Muhammad Yunus was awarded the Nobel Peace Prize for making the cell phone.

T or F   Yogi Bear said "It is always the simple that produces the marvelous."

T or F   The theme of Esther is "Return to Restore Worship and Morality."

T or F   Bridgetown is the capital of Barbados, which is in the continent of North America.

T or F   The saxophone was invented in 1840's by Adolphe Sax.

T or F   The theme of Job is "The sovereignty of God in human suffering."

REARRANGE

a. **the Books of the Bible in order:** Esther, 1st Chronicle, Job, Ezra, 2nd Chronicle, Nehemiah

1)_____ 2)_____ 3)_____

4)_____ 5)_____ 6)_____

b. **the largest countries by population:** Nigeria, Bangladesh, Pakistan, USA, Brazil, Japan, China, Russia, Indonesia, India

1) _____ 2) _____ 3) _____

4) _____ 5) _____ 6) _____

7) _____ 8) _____ 9) _____

10) _____

WRITE THE THEME OF THE FOLLOWING BOOKS:

a. 1st Chronicles _____

b. 2nd Chronicles _____

c. Ezra _____

d. Nehemiah _____

e. Esther _____

f. Job _____

MEMORIZE AND WRITE

Joshua 1:8 _____

_____

_____

ACTIVITY: ON A BLANK PIECE OF PAPER, DRAW YOUR FAVORITE MALE AND FEMALE ANIMAL PAIR.

Day 22 ~ The Tower of Babel

OPENING PRAYER

READ: Genesis 11:1-9

And the whole Earth was of one...

1) In which city was the tower built and why were bricks and mortar used? _____

_____

_____

2) What was the purpose of building the tower? _____

_____

3) What happened when God knew the people's intention? _____

_____

Explore God's World

MEMORY VERSES:

Psalm 139:14-15 "I will praise You, for I am fearfully and wonderfully made, marvelous are Your works, and that my soul knows very well. My frame was not hidden from You, when I was made in secret, and skillfully wrought in the lowest parts of the earth."

PSALMS	THEME
19th book of the Bible with 150 chapters	Israel's worship hymnal

For Your Information

FUN FACTS	THE TEN MOST POPULOUS CITIES OF THE WORLD (METROPOLITAN)	BELIZE
1. Baseball and Cricket are the only major sports where the defense has the ball. 2. The Spanish ritual of New Year's Eve is to eat 12 grapes at midnight. It is done in the hope of having 12 happy months in the coming year.	1) Tokyo, Japan 2) Jakarta, Indonesia 3) Seoul, South Korea 4) Delhi, India 5) Shanghai, China 6) Manila, Philippines 7) Karachi, Pakistan 8) New York, USA 9) San Paulo, Brazil 10) Mexico City, Mexico	...is in the continent of North America; Belmopan is the capital. The country is known for its September celebrations. Belize is the birthplace of chewing gum and Punta music. The nation provides the ideal home for more than 5000 species of plants and 100's species of animals.

GROUP DISCUSSION AND CLOSING PRAYER

"I am prepared for the worst, but hope for the best."

Benjamin Disraeli

Day 23 ~ Abram & Sarai

OPENING PRAYER
READ: Genesis 11:27, 31-32 and 12:1-20

Now the LORD had said unto...

1) What did God reveal to Abram? _____

_____

_____

2) What did Abram say to Sarai? _____

_____

3) What happened to the house of Pharaoh? _____

_____

Explore God's World

MEMORY VERSES:

Psalm 139:14-15 "I will praise You, for I am fearfully and wonderfully made, marvelous are Your works, and that my soul knows very well. My frame was not hidden from You, when I was made in secret, and skillfully wrought in the lowest parts of the earth."

PROVERBS	THEME
20th book of the Bible with 31 chapters	Wisdom

For Your Information

FUN FACTS	THE TEN MOST POPULOUS CITIES OF THE WORLD (METROPOLITAN)	BENIN
1. North Korea uses a fax machine to send threats to South Korea. 2. The idea of using a parachute to fall gently to the ground was written by Leonardo da Vinci. The first parachute was demonstrated in 1783 by Louis S. Lenormand of France.	1) Tokyo, Japan 2) Jakarta, Indonesia 3) Seoul, South Korea 4) Delhi, India 5) Shanghai, China 6) Manila, Philippines 7) Karachi, Pakistan 8) New York, USA 9) San Paulo, Brazil 10) Mexico City, Mexico	...is in the continent of Africa; Porto-Novo is the capital. The official language is French. However, indigenous languages, such as Fon and Yoruba, are commonly spoken. The largest religious group in Benin is Roman Catholicism.

GROUP DISCUSSION AND CLOSING PRAYER

"Wise men speak because they have something to say; Fools because they have to say something."

Plato

Day 24 ~ Abram & Lot Separated

OPENING PRAYER
READ: Genesis 13:5-18

And Lot also...

1) What caused the dispute between Abram and Lot and how did it end? _____
_____
_____

2) What evil things were the people of Sodom doing to displease the Lord? _____
_____

3) What do you know about Sodom? _____
_____

Explore God's World

MEMORY VERSES:

Psalm 139:14-15 "I will praise You, for I am fearfully and wonderfully made, marvelous are Your works, and that my soul knows very well. My frame was not hidden from You, when I was made in secret, and skillfully wrought in the lowest parts of the earth."

ECCLESIASTES	**THEME**
21st book of the Bible with 12 chapters	The futility of life; the importance of fearing Elohim

For Your Information

FUN FACTS	**THE TEN MOST POPULOUS CITIES OF THE WORLD (METROPOLITAN)**	**BHUTAN**
1. The Korean version of "LOL" is "KKK", which means "Hahaha." 2. Forensic scientists can determine a person's sex, age and race just by examining a single strand of hair.	1) Tokyo, Japan 2) Jakarta, Indonesia 3) Seoul, South Korea 4) Delhi, India 5) Shanghai, China 6) Manila, Philippines 7) Karachi, Pakistan 8) New York, USA 9) San Paulo, Brazil 10) Mexico City, Mexico	...is in the continent of Asia; Thimphu is the capital. Bhutan is also known as the kingdom of Bhutan. The landlocked country is predominantly Buddhist, with Hinduism as the 2nd largest religion. Bhutan has a rich primate life with rare species, such as the golden langur. The currency is Bhutanese ngultrum.

GROUP DISCUSSION AND CLOSING PRAYER

"Start where you are. Use what you have. Do what you can."

Arthur Ashe

Day 25 ~ Hagar & Ishmael

OPENING PRAYER
READ: Genesis 16:1-16

Now Sarai Abram's wife bore...

1) Who was Hagar? _____

_____

_____

2) What did Sarai tell Abram to do about Hagar? _____

_____

3) What did the angel of the LORD say to Hagar? _____

_____

Explore God's World

MEMORY VERSES:

Psalm 139:14-15 "I will praise You, for I am fearfully and wonderfully made, marvelous are Your works, and that my soul knows very well. My frame was not hidden from You, when I was made in secret, and skillfully wrought in the lowest parts of the earth."

SONG OF SOLOMON	**THEME**
22nd book of the Bible with 8 chapters	The beauty of love and marriage

For Your Information

FUN FACTS	THE TEN MOST POPULOUS CITIES OF THE WORLD (METROPOLITAN)	BOLIVIA
1. Cuban rescue workers use sniffer rabbits to find people in collapsed buildings.	1) Tokyo, Japan 2) Jakarta, Indonesia 3) Seoul, South Korea 4) Delhi, India 5) Shanghai, China 6) Manila, Philippines 7) Karachi, Pakistan 8) New York, USA 9) San Paulo, Brazil 10) Mexico City, Mexico	...is in the continent of South America; Sucre is the capital. The country is named after Simon Bolivar, a leader in the Spanish American wars of independence. The Constitution recognizes 37 official languages, aside from Spanish.
2. Leonardo da Vinci made detailed sketches of the airplane, the helicopter, the parachute, the submarine, the armored car, and the ballista rapid-fire guns.		

GROUP DISCUSSION AND CLOSING PRAYER

"You change your life by changing your heart."

Max Lucado

Day 26 ~ Abram to Abraham

OPENING PRAYER
READ: Genesis 17:1-25

And when Abram...

1) Why did God change their names? Explain the meanings of the names. _____
_____

_____

2) What kind of covenant did God make with Abraham? _____
_____

3) What did Abraham and all the men of his household do?_____
_____

Explore God's World

MEMORY VERSES:

Psalm 139:14-15 "I will praise You, for I am fearfully and wonderfully made, marvelous are Your works, and that my soul knows very well. My frame was not hidden from You, when I was made in secret, and skillfully wrought in the lowest parts of the earth."

ISAIAH	**THEME**
23rd book of the Bible with 66 chapters	Yahweh is salvation

For Your Information

FUN FACTS	**THE TEN MOST POPULOUS CITIES OF THE WORLD (METROPOLITAN)**	**BOSNIA AND HERZEGOVINA (ONE COUNTRY)**
1. Salmon sushi was originally introduced to Japan by Norway. 2. There is more real lemon juice in Lemon Pledge furniture polish than in Country Time Lemonade.	1) Tokyo, Japan 2) Jakarta, Indonesia 3) Seoul, South Korea 4) Delhi, India 5) Shanghai, China 6) Manila, Philippines 7) Karachi, Pakistan 8) New York, USA 9) San Paulo, Brazil 10) Mexico City, Mexico	...is in the continent of Europe; Sarajevo is the capital. Coffee drinking is a favorite pass-time and part of the culture. Many spices in moderate quantities are used in the cuisine. Bosnia was one of the six republics in former Yugoslavia.

GROUP DISCUSSION AND CLOSING PRAYER

"We know what we are, but know not what we may be."

William Shakespeare

Day 27 ~ The Birth of Isaac

OPENING PRAYER
READ: Genesis 21:1-91

And the LORD visited...

1) When Isaac was born what was Ishmael's attitude towards Isaac? _____

_____

_____

2) What sacrifice did Abraham offer and how was God's heart touched? _____

_____

3) What is so important in Genesis 22:15-17? _____

_____

Explore God's World

MEMORY VERSES:

Psalm 139:14-15 "I will praise You, for I am fearfully and wonderfully made, marvelous are Your works, and that my soul knows very well. My frame was not hidden from You, when I was made in secret, and skillfully wrought in the lowest parts of the earth."

JEREMIAH	THEME
24th book of the Bible with 52 chapters	Yahweh's justice: the fall of Jerusalem

For Your Information

FUN FACTS	THE TEN MOST POPULOUS CITIES OF THE WORLD (METROPOLITAN)	BOTSWANA
1. Every year, nearly 4 million cats are eaten in China as a delicacy. 2. According to the Wildlife Conservation Society, the perfume "Obsession for men" attracts jaguars, pumas and other wildlife.	1) Tokyo, Japan 2) Jakarta, Indonesia 3) Seoul, South Korea 4) Delhi, India 5) Shanghai, China 6) Manila, Philippines 7) Karachi, Pakistan 8) New York, USA 9) San Paulo, Brazil 10) Mexico City, Mexico	...is in the continent of Africa; Gaborone is the capital. The Jwaneng Diamond Mine, is the world's richest diamond mine. The citizens refer to themselves as "Batswana." The Botswana faces two major environmental problems: drought and desertification.

GROUP DISCUSSION AND CLOSING PRAYER

"Faith is to believe what we do not see, and the reward of this faith is to see what we believe."

St. Augustine

Day 28 ~ Week in Review

MEMORIZE AND WRITE

Psalm 139:14-15 _____

_____

_____

TRUE OR FALSE — Circle T for true or F for false

T or F   The largest religious group in Benin is Roman Catholicism.

T or F   Hagar was Sarah's Egyptian maidservant.

T or F   Ishmael means, "my friend."

T or F   The 6th most populous city is Manila, Philippines.

T or F   Abraham means the called one.

T or F   Yahweh is Salvation in the theme of the book of Isaiah.

T or F   The two cities destroyed were Sodom and Gomorrah.

T or F   When Lot's wife looked back she became a pillar of cement.

T or F   Brazil is in the continent of South America.

T or F   Isaac is the son of the covenant.

WRITE THE THEME OF THE FOLLOWING BOOKS

a. Psalms _____

b. Proverbs _____

c. Ecclesiastes _____

d. Song of Solomon _____

e. Isaiah _____

f. Jeremiah _____

NAME THE TEN MOST POPULOUS CITIES IN THE WORLD _____

_____

_____

_____

MATCH THE FOLLOWING

_____ a. Song of Solomon

_____ b. Bhutan

_____ c. Proverbs

_____ d. Isaiah

_____ e. Bosnia and Herzegovina

_____ f. Botswana

_____ g. Jeremiah

_____ h. Bolivia

_____ i. Psalms

_____ j. Belize

_____ k. Ecclesiastes

_____ l. Benin

1. The Futility of Life; The Importance of Fearing Elohim

2. Sarajevo

3. Belmopan

4. Thimphu

5. The Fall of Jerusalem

6. Porto-Novo

7. The Beauty of Love and Marriage

8. Israel's Worship Hymnal

9. Gaborone

10. Yahweh is Salvation

11. Wisdom

12. Sucre

WHAT WERE THE CONSEQUENCES OF ABRAHAM TRYING TO FULFILL GOD'S PROMISE FOR A SON INSTEAD OF WAITING ON GOD TO FULFILL IT?

_____

_____

_____

_____

Coloring Activity

Note, you may make copies of this page to color if multiple family members in the same household want to color the illustration.

Day 29 ~ Eliezer & Rebekah

OPENING PRAYER

READ: Genesis 24:1-17 and 50-57

Now Abraham was old...

1) Why did Abraham send Eliezer, his servant, to Mesopotamia? _____
_____
_____

2) What did Laban and Bethuel say to Eliezer? _____
_____

3) What took place in verses 56-57? _____
_____

Explore God's World

MEMORY VERSES:

Romans 5:1 "Therefore, having been justified by faith, we have peace with God, through our Lord Jesus Christ."

Romans 10:13 "For whoever calls on the name of the Lord shall be saved."

LAMENTATIONS	THEME
25th book of the Bible with 5 chapters	The pain of divine discipline

For Your Information

FUN FACTS	THE TOP TEN LONGEST RIVERS OF THE WORLD	BRAZIL
1. The King James Bible has inspired the lyrics of more pop songs than any other book. 2. There's a cruise ship named "The World" on which, residents permanently live as it travels around the globe.	1) Nile in Africa 2) Amazon in South America 3) Mississippi-Missouri-Red Rock in USA 4) Chang Jiang (Yangtze) in China 5) Ob in Russia 6) Huang Ho (Yellow) in China 7) Yenisei in Russia 8) Parana in South America 9) Irtysh in Russia 10) Zaire in Congo	...is in the continent of South America; Brasilia is the capital. It is the largest producer of coffee in the world. Brazil is home to the Amazon Rainforest. The country is the only Portuguese-speaking nation in the Americas. Football is the most popular sport.

GROUP DISCUSSION AND CLOSING PRAYER

"The greatest gift that you can give to others is the gift of unconditional love and acceptance."

Brian Tracy

Day 30 ~ Esau & Jacob

OPENING PRAYER

READ: Genesis 25:1-11 and 23-34

Now it came to pass...

1) Who died when he was 175 years old? _____

_____

2) What did the Lord say to Rebekah in verse 23? _____

_____

3) Why did Esau sell his birth right and to whom?_____

_____

_____

Explore God's World

MEMORY VERSES:

Romans 5:1 "Therefore, having been justified by faith, we have peace with God, through our Lord Jesus Christ."

Romans 10:13 "For whoever calls on the name of the Lord shall be saved."

EZEKIEL	THEME
26th book of the Bible with 48 chapters	Judgment and restoration until all know I Am Yahweh

For Your Information

FUN FACTS	THE TOP TEN LONGEST RIVERS OF THE WORLD	BRUNEI
1. According to the gaming law, casinos have to stock enough cash to cover chips on the "floor." 2. Apple's co-founder Roland Wayne sold his 10% share in 1976 for $800. Today, it's worth nearly $60 billion.	1) Nile in Africa 2) Amazon in South America 3) Mississippi-Missouri-Red Rock in USA 4) Chang Jiang (Yangtze) in China 5) Ob in Russia 6) Huang Ho (Yellow) in China 7) Yenisei in Russia 8) Parana in South America 9) Irtysh in Russia 10) Zaire in Congo	...is in the continent of Asia; Bandar Seri Begawan is the capital. The official language is Malay. The IMF estimated in 2011 that Brunei was one of two countries (the other being Libya), with a public debt at 0% of the national GDP. Brunei is the 4th largest producer of oil in Southeast Asia and the 9th largest exporter of the liquefied natural gas in the world.

GROUP DISCUSSION AND CLOSING PRAYER

"He that can have patience can have what he will."

Benjamin Franklin

Day 31 ~ Jacob's Vision & Vow

OPENING PRAYER
READ: Genesis 28:1-22

Then Isaac called Jacob...

1) What was included in Jacob's blessing? _____
_____
_____

2) Who was Mahalath and how was she related to Ishmael? _____
_____

3) What was the importance of Bethel? _____
_____

Explore God's World

MEMORY VERSES:

Romans 5:1 "Therefore, having been justified by faith, we have peace with God, through our Lord Jesus Christ."

Romans 10:13 "For whoever calls on the name of the Lord shall be saved."

DANIEL	THEME
27th book of the Bible with 12 chapters	The sovereignty of God over the nations

For Your Information

FUN FACTS	THE TOP TEN LONGEST RIVERS OF THE WORLD	BULGARIA
1. Coffee was originally called "Arabian Wine" when it was first brought to Europe. 2. Zoroastrians in India leave the bodies of the dead outdoors to be consumed by vultures.	1) Nile in Africa 2) Amazon in South America 3) Mississippi-Missouri-Red Rock in USA 4) Chang Jiang (Yangtze) in China 5) Ob in Russia 6) Huang Ho (Yellow) in China 7) Yenisei in Russia 8) Parana in South America 9) Irtysh in Russia 10) Zaire in Congo	...is in the continent of Europe; Sofia is the capital. The country borders Greece, Turkey, Macedonia, Serbia and Romania. Bulgaria is one of the world's biggest winemakers. The first electronic computer, digital watch and car airbag were invented in Bulgaria.

GROUP DISCUSSION AND CLOSING PRAYER

"A real Christian is a person who can give his pet parrot to the town gossip."

Billy Graham

Day 32 ~ Jacob Meets Rachel, Laban, & Leah

OPENING PRAYER
READ: Genesis 29:5-35

Then he said to...

1) What was the relationship between Jacob and Laban? _____
_____
_____

2) Whom did Jacob love and who was his first wife? _____
_____

3) How many years did Jacob work to have Rachel as his wife? _____
_____

Explore God's World

MEMORY VERSES:
Romans 5:1 "Therefore, having been justified by faith, we have peace with God, through our Lord Jesus Christ."
Romans 10:13 "For whoever calls on the name of the Lord shall be saved."

HOSEA	THEME
28th book of the Bible with 14 chapters	Yahweh's lawsuit against His adulterous wife, Israel, to reclaim her, for He loves her

For Your Information

FUN FACTS	THE TOP TEN LONGEST RIVERS OF THE WORLD	BURKINA FASO (REPUBLIC OF UPPER VOLTA)
1. Alexander Graham Bell invented the telephone (with Thomas Watson) in 1876. 2. Marion Donovan invented the disposable diaper in 1950. Her first leak-proof diaper was a plastic-lined cloth diaper.	1) Nile in Africa 2) Amazon in South America 3) Mississippi-Missouri-Red Rock in USA 4) Chang Jiang (Yangtze) in China 5) Ob in Russia 6) Huang Ho (Yellow) in China 7) Yenisei in Russia 8) Parana in South America 9) Irtysh in Russia 10) Zaire in Congo	...is in the continent of Africa; Ouagadougou is the capital. French is the official language and football is very popular here. Schooling costs approximately $97 USD per student per year; the amount is far above the means of most Burkinabe families.

GROUP DISCUSSION AND CLOSING PRAYER

"Rivers know this: there is no hurry. We shall get there someday."

A.A. Milne

Day 33 ~ Jacob's Wages & Success

OPENING PRAYER
READ: Genesis 30:3-7 and 23-43

So she said...

1) Why did Jacob say "Am I in the place of God"? Who was Bilhah? _____

_____

_____

2) How did God favor Rachel? _____

_____

3) What was the agreement between Laban and Jacob? _____

_____

Explore God's World

MEMORY VERSES:

Romans 5:1 "Therefore, having been justified by faith, we have peace with God, through our Lord Jesus Christ."

Romans 10:13 "For whoever calls on the name of the Lord shall be saved."

JOEL	THEME
29th book of the Bible with 3 chapters	The Day of the LORD

For Your Information

FUN FACTS	THE TOP TEN LONGEST RIVERS OF THE WORLD	BURUNDI
1. John F. Kennedy was buried without his brain because it was lost during the autopsy. 2. Technically the almond is not a nut. It is actually the pit of a fruit related to peaches, plums and apricots.	1) Nile in Africa 2) Amazon in South America 3) Mississippi-Missouri-Red Rock in USA 4) Chang Jiang (Yangtze) in China 5) Ob in Russia 6) Huang Ho (Yellow) in China 7) Yenisei in Russia 8) Parana in South America 9) Irtysh in Russia 10) Zaire in Congo	...is in the continent of Africa; Bujumbura is the capital. The typical Burundian meal consists of sweet potatoes, corn, and peas. Drumming is an important part of the cultural heritage and the national sport is Soccer. The country is still one of the five poorest countries in the world.

GROUP DISCUSSION AND CLOSING PRAYER

"We can easily forgive a child who is afraid of the dark; the real tragedy of life is when men are afraid of the light."

Plato

Day 34 ~ Israel

OPENING PRAYER
READ: Genesis 32:7-32

So Jacob was...

1) How did Jacob feel when he reunited with Esau in verse 7? _____

_____

_____

2) What was Jacob's prayer to the Lord? _____

_____

3) What was the result of the wrestling and what was Jacob's new name? _____

_____

Explore God's World

MEMORY VERSES:

Romans 5:1 "Therefore, having been justified by faith, we have peace with God, through our Lord Jesus Christ."

Romans 10:13 "For whoever calls on the name of the Lord shall be saved."

AMOS	**THEME**
30th book of the Bible with 9 chapters	Israel's inevitable judgment for idolatry and injustice

For Your Information

FUN FACTS	THE TOP TEN LONGEST RIVERS OF THE WORLD	CAMBODIA (KINGDOM OF CAMBODIA)
1. Leonardo Da Vinci was the first to explain why the sky is blue. 2. Army ants are used as natural sutures because their jaws are so powerful. American Indigenous peoples use army ants by forcing ants to bite a wound, then breaking off the ants' bodies, leaving the head attached to the wound.	1) Nile in Africa 2) Amazon in South America 3) Mississippi-Missouri-Red Rock in USA 4) Chang Jiang (Yangtze) in China 5) Ob in Russia 6) Huang Ho (Yellow) in China 7) Yenisei in Russia 8) Parana in South America 9) Irtysh in Russia 10) Zaire in Congo	...is in the continent of Asia; Phnom Penh is the capital. Cambodia's ancient name is Kambuja or Kampuchea, the most common former name of Cambodia, means "Golden Land" or "Land of Peace and Prosperity." Both names applied at separate times in history. The minority groups include Vietnamese, Chinese, Chams, and 30 hill tribes.

GROUP DISCUSSION AND CLOSING PRAYER

"Patience is bitter, but its fruit is sweet."

Aristotle

Day 35 ~ Week in Review

TRUE OR FALSE — Circle T for true or F for false

T or F   Lamentations is the 24th book of the Bible with 7 chapters.

T or F   Rachel was Jacob's first wife.

T or F   Parana River is in China and Ob in Russia.

T or F   Esau sold his birth rights because he was going to a different land.

T or F   The theme of Hosea is "The Sovereignty of God Over the Nations."

T or F   Cambodia is one of the five poorest countries in the world.

T or F   Amos is the 30th book of the Bible in the Old Testament with 9 chapters.

T or F   Sofia is the capital of Burundi.

T or F   A.A. Milne said, "Patience is bitter, but its fruit is sweet."

T or F   The theme of book of Joel is "The Day of the Lord."

CIRCLE THE CORRECT ANSWERS

a. The theme of Lamentations is
   1. To please God in all circumstances.
   2. The Lord's Day is coming soon.
   3. The pain of Divine Discipline.

b. The typical Burundian meal consists of
   1. bake potatoes and green peas.
   2. sweet potatoes, corn and peas.
   3. fried rice with sweet and sour chicken.

c. Cambodia's ancient name is "Kambuja" or Kampuchea, which means
   1. "the land of golden sun."
   2. "golden land" or "Land of peace and prosperity."
   3. "the land of the saints."

d. Which is the 4th largest producer of oil in South Asia?
   1. Bangladesh
   2. Brunei
   3. "the land of the saints."

FILL IN THE BLANKS

a. French is the _____ language and _____ is very _____ in Burkina Faso.

b. The _____ groups in Cambodia includes _____, Chinese, _____, and 30 hill _____.

c. Bulgaria invented the 1st _____, _____ watch and _____.

d. Brunei is the 4th _____ producer of oil in _____ Asia and 9th largest _____ of liquefied gas in the _____.

e. Burundi is _____ one of the _____ poorest _____ in the world.

f. The _____ Nile is in Africa and the _____ Yenisei is in _____.

g. Brazil is the only _____ speaking _____ in _____.

h. Daniel's theme is the _____ of _____ over the _____.

i. Ezekiel's theme is the _____ and _____ until all _____ I am _____.

MEMORIZE AND WRITE

Romans 5:1 _____

_____

_____

Romans 10:3 _____

_____

_____

HOW DID JACOB OBTAIN THE BIRTHRIGHT, AND HOW DID JACOB ALSO RECEIVE THE EXTRA BLESSING FROM HIS FATHER?

_____

_____

_____

_____

_____

*Note, you may make copies of this page to color if multiple family members in
the same household want to color the illustration.*

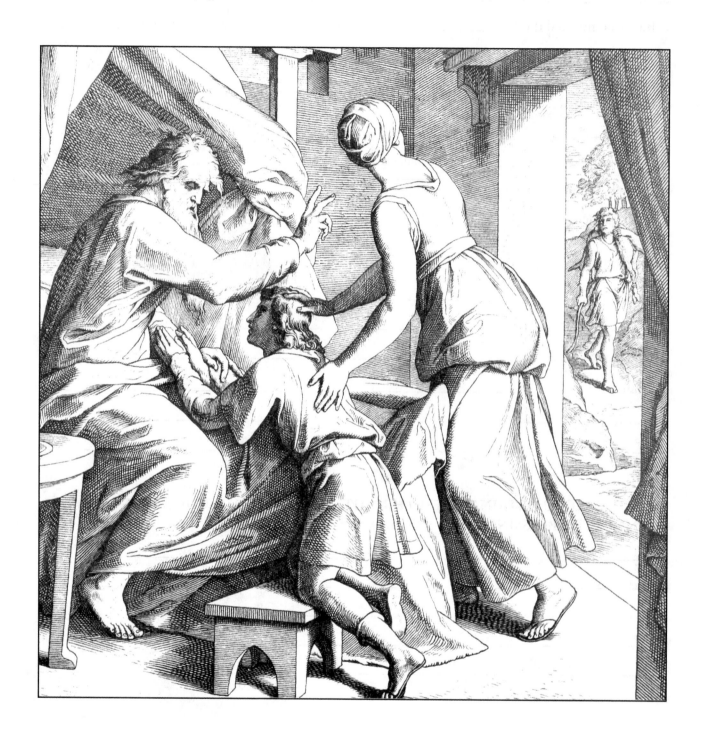

Day 36 ~ Joseph

OPENING PRAYER
READ: Genesis 37:1-36

Now Jacob dwelt in...

1) Of his sons, whom did Jacob love the most?_____
_____
_____

2) What was Joseph's dream and what was his brothers' reaction to it?_____
_____

3) What action did the brothers take against Joseph?_____
_____

Explore God's World

MEMORY VERSES:
Romans 8:38-39 "For I am persuaded that neither death nor life, nor angels, nor principalities, nor powers, nor things present, nor things to come, nor height, nor depth, nor any other created thing, shall be able to separate us from the love of God which is in Christ Jesus, our Lord."

OBADIAH	THEME
31st book of the Bible with 1 chapter	The downfall of Edom

For Your Information

FUN FACTS	THE TOP TEN LONGEST RIVERS OF THE WORLD	CAMEROON
1. Salmon sushi was originally introduced to Japan by Norway. 2. A mother's body makes the perfect milk for her baby. Breast milk changes its nutritional profile as the baby grows.	1) Nile in Africa 2) Amazon in South America 3) Mississippi-Missouri-Red Rock in USA 4) Chang Jiang (Yangtze) in China 5) Ob in Russia 6) Huang Ho (Yellow) in China 7) Yenisei in Russia 8) Parana in South America 9) Irtysh in Russia 10) Zaire in Congo	...is in the continent of Africa; Yaoundé is the capital. The country is famous for its native styles of music, particularly makossa and bikutsi. French and English are the official languages, but there are over 200 different linguistic groups.

GROUP DISCUSSION AND CLOSING PRAYER

"I try to embrace people with love, unconditional love, like Christ did."
Thomas Kinkade

Day 37 ~ Prison & the Dreams

OPENING PRAYER

READ: Genesis 39:6-20 and 40:5-19

Thus he left...

1) What happened between Potiphar's wife and Joseph? _____

_____

_____

2) Who falsely accused Joseph and where did he end up? _____

_____

3) What were the dreams of the butler and the baker? _____

_____

Explore God's World

MEMORY VERSES:

Romans 8:38-39 "For I am persuaded that neither death nor life, nor angels, nor principalities, nor powers, nor things present, nor things to come, nor height, nor depth, nor any other created thing, shall be able to separate us from the love of God which is in Christ Jesus, our Lord."

JONAH	THEME
32nd book of the Bible with 4 chapters	Mercy amid judgment

For Your Information

FUN FACTS	THE TOP TEN LONGEST RIVERS OF THE WORLD	CANADA
Bar codes (Universal Product Codes or UPC's) are small coded labels that contain information about the item they are attached to. The information is contained in a numerical code, usually containing 12 digits. UPC's are easily scanned by laser beams.	1) Nile in Africa 2) Amazon in South America 3) Mississippi-Missouri-Red Rock in USA 4) Chang Jiang (Yangtze) in China 5) Ob in Russia 6) Huang Ho (Yellow) in China 7) Yenisei in Russia 8) Parana in South America 9) Irtysh in Russia 10) Zaire in Congo	...is in the continent of North America; Ottawa is the capital. The name came from the St. Lawrence Iroquoian word kanata, meaning "village" or "settlement." Canada is the world's 2nd largest country by total area that shares a common border with the US. The country has around 31,700 large fresh water lakes. The two official languages are English and French.

GROUP DISCUSSION AND CLOSING PRAYER

"Why is patience so important? Because it makes us pay attention."

Paulo Coelho

Day 38 ~ Pharaoh's Dream Interpretation

OPENING PRAYER
READ: Genesis 41:1-40

Then it came to pass...

1) What was Pharaoh's dreams? _____
_____
_____

2) What did the chief butler say about Joseph? _____
_____

3) Who interpreted the dreams and what was his reward in return?_____
_____

Explore God's World

MEMORY VERSES:

Romans 8:38-39 "For I am persuaded that neither death nor life, nor angels, nor principalities, nor powers, nor things present, nor things to come, nor height, nor depth, nor any other created thing, shall be able to separate us from the love of God which is in Christ Jesus, our Lord."

MICAH	THEME
33rd book of the Bible with 7 chapters	Yahweh's court case against Israel and Judah

For Your Information

FUN FACTS	THE TOP TEN LONGEST RIVERS OF THE WORLD	CENTRAL AFRICAN REPUBLIC
1. Bangkok is known by the Thai people as "Krung Thep," which means "City of Angels." 2. The Lion used in the original MGM logo killed its trainer and two assistants the day after the logo was filmed.	1) Nile in Africa 2) Amazon in South America 3) Mississippi-Missouri-Red Rock in USA 4) Chang Jiang (Yangtze) in China 5) Ob in Russia 6) Huang Ho (Yellow) in China 7) Yenisei in Russia 8) Parana in South America 9) Irtysh in Russia 10) Zaire in Congo	…is in the continent of Africa; Bangui is the capital. French and Sango are official languages. The Republic is divided into over 80 ethnic groups, each having its own language. 68% of the marriages fall under the category of child marriages.

GROUP DISCUSSION AND CLOSING PRAYER

"One of the penalties for refusing to participate in politics is that you end up being governed by your inferiors."

Plato

Day 39 ~ The Union of Benjamin with Joseph

OPENING PRAYER
READ: Genesis 43:6-31

Now Joseph was...

1) In order for the brothers to get more food, what did Joseph demand from his brothers?_____
_____
_____

2) What was put back in the sacks of Israel's sons. What did they do with the unexpected items?____
_____
_____

3) What was Joseph's reaction to seeing his brother Benjamin?_____
_____

Explore God's World

MEMORY VERSES:

Romans 8:38-39 "For I am persuaded that neither death nor life, nor angels, nor principalities, nor powers, nor things present, nor things to come, nor height, nor depth, nor any other created thing, shall be able to separate us from the love of God which is in Christ Jesus, our Lord."

NAHUM	THEME
34th book of the Bible with 3 chapters	The judgment of Nineveh

For Your Information

FUN FACTS	THE TOP TEN LONGEST RIVERS OF THE WORLD	CHAD
1. A baby octopus is about the size of a flea at birth. 2. After the Department of Defense, Walt Disney World is the second largest purchaser of explosives in the United States.	1) Nile in Africa 2) Amazon in South America 3) Mississippi-Missouri-Red Rock in USA 4) Chang Jiang (Yangtze) in China 5) Ob in Russia 6) Huang Ho (Yellow) in China 7) Yenisei in Russia 8) Parana in South America 9) Irtysh in Russia 10) Zaire in Congo	...is in the continent of Africa; N'Djamena is the capital. Having a large desert climate, Chad is referred to as the "Dead Heart of Africa." Lake Chad is Africa's 2nd largest wetland. With over 200 tribes living in the area, the wetland aids in creating diverse social structures. As the people are connected only by wetland.

GROUP DISCUSSION AND CLOSING PRAYER

"The key to everything is patience. You get the chicken by hatching the egg, not by smashing it."

Arnold H. Glasgow

Day 40 ~ *The Final Test*

OPENING PRAYER
READ: Genesis 44:1-34

And he commanded the...

1) Why did Joseph instruct his stewards to follow his brothers?_____
_____
_____

2) What was put in Benjamin's sack and why did Judah intercede on his brother's behalf?_____
_____

3) What did the brothers tell Joseph if Benjamin did not return with them to their father?_____
_____

Explore God's World

MEMORY VERSES:

Romans 8:38-39 "For I am persuaded that neither death nor life, nor angels, nor principalities, nor powers, nor things present, nor things to come, nor height, nor depth, nor any other created thing, shall be able to separate us from the love of God which is in Christ Jesus, our Lord."

HABAKKUK	THEME
35th book of the Bible with 3 chapters	Faith amidst perplexity

For Your Information

FUN FACTS	THE TOP TEN LONGEST RIVERS OF THE WORLD	CHILE
1. More people are allergic to cow's milk than any other food. 2. Before the invention of the hair dryer, it was common for men and women to dry their hair using a vacuum cleaner.	1) Nile in Africa 2) Amazon in South America 3) Mississippi-Missouri-Red Rock in USA 4) Chang Jiang (Yangtze) in China 5) Ob in Russia 6) Huang Ho (Yellow) in China 7) Yenisei in Russia 8) Parana in South America 9) Irtysh in Russia 10) Zaire in Congo	...is in the continent of South America; Santiago is the capital. Chile is one of South America's most stable and prosperous nations. There are several indigenous languages, but the official language is Spanish. The most popular sport is football.

GROUP DISCUSSION AND CLOSING PRAYER

"But groundless hope, like unconditional love, is the only kind worth having."

John Perry Barlow

Day 41 ~ Joseph Makes Himself Known to His Brothers

OPENING PRAYER
READ: Genesis 45:1-28

Then Joseph could...

1) Describe how Joseph told his brothers that he is the one whom they sold into slavery?_____
_____
_____

2) What was Pharaoh's response upon learning that Joseph was reunited with his brothers?_____
_____

3) What did Joseph give to his brothers and father? _____
_____

Explore God's World

MEMORY VERSES:

Romans 8:38-39 "For I am persuaded that neither death nor life, nor angels, nor principalities, nor powers, nor things present, nor things to come, nor height, nor depth, nor any other created thing, shall be able to separate us from the love of God which is in Christ Jesus, our Lord."

ZEPHANIAH	THEME
36th book of the Bible with 3 chapters	The day of the LORD: Yahweh's wrath and reign over the nations

For Your Information

FUN FACTS	THE TOP TEN LONGEST RIVERS OF THE WORLD	CHINA
1. The firefly is not actually a fly, but a beetle. 2. The safety pin was invented by Walter Hunt on April 10,1849. It was made by twisting a length of wire.	1) Nile in Africa 2) Amazon in South America 3) Mississippi-Missouri-Red Rock in USA 4) Chang Jiang (Yangtze) in China 5) Ob in Russia 6) Huang Ho (Yellow) in China 7) Yenisei in Russia 8) Parana in South America 9) Irtysh in Russia 10) Zaire in Congo	...is in the continent of Asia; Beijing is the capital. The world's most populous country, China is also the world's largest exporter and importer of goods. The country is a recognized nuclear weapons state and has the world's largest standing army; China has the world's 2nd largest defense budget

GROUP DISCUSSION AND CLOSING PRAYER

"In fact, when care appears, unconditional love often vanishes."

Martha Beck

Day 42 ~ Week in Review

WRITE THE THEME OF THE FOLLOWING BOOKS

a. Obadiah _____

b. Jonah _____

c. Micah _____

d. Nahum _____

e. Habakkuk _____

f. Zephaniah _____

TRUE OR FALSE — Circle T for true or F for false

T or F   Cameroon is home to over 200 different linguistic groups.

T or F   Lhotse is the world's 7th highest mountain in the world.

T or F   Jonah is the 32nd book of the Bible with 4 chapters.

T or F   Canada has 31,700 large fresh water lakes.

T or F   Bangui is the capital of Chad.

T or F   Chile's official language is Spanish.

T or F   China is the world's 4th largest exporter and importer of goods.

T or F   K2 (Mount Godwin Austen) is in Pakistan and China.

T or F   Zephaniah is the 36th book of the Bible with 3 chapters.

T or F   Chad's largest desert is also known as the "Dead Heart of Africa."

CIRCLE THE CORRECT ANSWERS

a. Mount Everest is in

    1.   Japan and South Korea

    2.   Nepal and Tibet

    3.   India and Nepal

b. Ottawa is the capital of

    1.   Cameroon

    2.   Central African Republic

    3.   Canada

   c. Micah is the

      1. 49th book of the Bible with 10 chapters

      2. 33rd book of the Bible with 7 chapters

      3. 31st book of the Bible with 8 chapters

   d. The theme of Nahum is

      1. The judgment of Nineveh

      2. The wrath of God on Nineveh

      3. Faith amidst Perplexity

   e. Chile's most popular sport is

      1. billiard

      2. cricket

      3. football

MEMORIZE AND WRITE

Romans 8:38-39 _____

_____

_____

_____

_____

LIST SOME OF THE DREAMS THAT JOSEPH INTERPRETED AND HOW GOD USED THOSE DREAMS IN JOSEPH, THE PEOPLE OF ISRAEL, AND THE EGYPTIANS

_____

_____

_____

_____

_____

Joseph's Coat of Many Colors Coloring Activity

Note, you may make copies of this page to color if multiple family members in the same household want to color the illustration.

Day 43 ~ The Suffering of the Israelites in Egypt

OPENING PRAYER
READ: Exodus 1:1-22

Now these are the...

1) Name the sons of Israel who came to Egypt. _____
_____
_____

2) How did the new king who didn't know Joseph treat the Israelites? _____
_____

3) What conversation took place between the Egyptian king and the midwives? _____
_____

Explore God's World

MEMORY VERSES:

Romans 8:1 "There is therefore now no condemnation to those who are in Christ Jesus, who do not walk according to the flesh, but according to the Spirit."

Romans 6:23 "For the wages of sin is death, but the gift of God is eternal life in Christ Jesus, our Lord."

HAGGAI	THEME
37th book of the Bible with 2 chapters	Rebuilding the temple before the blessing

For Your Information

FUN FACTS	THE TOP TEN WIDELY SPOKEN LANGUAGES IN THE WORLD	COLOMBIA
1. Water itself does not conduct electricity, but the impurities found in water do. 2. The White House was originally called the "Presidential Palace." It was renamed "The White House" by President Theodore Roosevelt in 1901.	1) Mandarin-Chinese 2) English 3) Hindustani 4) Spanish 5) Russian 6) Arabic 7) Bengali 8) Portuguese 9) Malay-Indonesia 10) French	...is in the continent of South America; Bogota is the capital. It was named after Christopher Columbus and is famous for beautifully preserved ancient ruins and colonial towns. Columbia has between 40,000-45,000 plant species and over 1,900 species of bird.

GROUP DISCUSSION AND CLOSING PRAYER

"I have held many things in my hand and I've lost them all, but whatever I have placed in God's I still hold."

Martin Luther

Day 44 ~ Moses' Birth & His Early Years

OPENING PRAYER
READ: Exodus 2:1-22

And a man of the...

1) Who was born in Levi's household, and what did the parents do with the child? _____

_____

_____

2) Who nursed the child, and what name was he given? _____

_____

3) What caused Moses to flee to Midian? _____

_____

Explore God's World

MEMORY VERSES:

Romans 8:1 "There is therefore now no condemnation to those who are in Christ Jesus, who do not walk according to the flesh, but according to the Spirit."

Romans 6:23 "For the wages of sin is death, but the gift of God is eternal life in Christ Jesus, our Lord."

ZECHARIAH	THEME
38th book of the Bible with 14 chapters	Israel's prophetic future

For Your Information

FUN FACTS	THE TOP TEN WIDELY SPOKEN LANGUAGES IN THE WORLD	COMOROS
1. The skin that covers the tip of your elbow is called a "wenis." 2. John S. Thurman invented the gasoline powered vacuum cleaner (which he called the "pneumatic carpet renovator") in 1899.	1) Mandarin-Chinese 2) English 3) Hindustani 4) Spanish 5) Russian 6) Arabic 7) Bengali 8) Portuguese 9) Malay-Indonesia 10) French	…is in the continent of Africa; Moroni is the capital. The three official languages are Comorian, Arabic, and French. One of the world's poorest countries, Comoros is the world's largest producer of ylang-ylang flowers, used for making a fragrant oil of the same name, and a large producer of vanilla.

GROUP DISCUSSION AND CLOSING PRAYER

"Upwards to heaven! Nearer to God!"

Charles H. Spurgeon

Day 45 ~ Moses' First Revelation from God

OPENING PRAYER
READ: Exodus 3:1-22

Now Moses was...

1) What happened in Horeb, the mountain of God? _____

_____

_____

2) What did the Lord say to Moses about His people? _____

_____

3) What can we learn in verses 14-16? _____

_____

Explore God's World

MEMORY VERSES:

Romans 8:1 "There is therefore now no condemnation to those who are in Christ Jesus, who do not walk according to the flesh, but according to the Spirit."

Romans 6:23 "For the wages of sin is death, but the gift of God is eternal life in Christ Jesus, our Lord."

MALACHI	THEME
39th book of the Bible with 4 chapters	Israel against Yahweh

For Your Information

FUN FACTS	THE TOP TEN WIDELY SPOKEN LANGUAGES IN THE WORLD	CONGO (REPUBLIC OF THE)
1. Nepal is the only country that has a non-rectangular flag. It is asymmetrical. 2. The same part of the brain that responds to fearful situations also shows a heightened response in children with high math anxiety.	1) Mandarin-Chinese 2) English 3) Hindustani 4) Spanish 5) Russian 6) Arabic 7) Bengali 8) Portuguese 9) Malay-Indonesia 10) French	...is in the continent of Africa; Brazzaville is the capital. The country is the world's largest producer of cobalt ore, copper and diamonds. Congo is bursting with natural geographic formations, from vast wilderness to virgin rainforests, from wild rivers to active volcanoes.

GROUP DISCUSSION AND CLOSING PRAYER

"Faith is not a sense, nor sight, nor reason, but simply taking God at His words."

Christmas Evans

Day 46 ~ Moses' Initial Unwillingness

OPENING PRAYER
READ: 4:1-31

Now Moses was...

1) What was Moses' response to the Lord's calling? _____

_____

_____

2) Who was Aaron, and what did the Lord tell him to do? _____

_____

3) What did Aaron's "rod" do in front of the Pharaoh? _____

_____

Explore God's World

MEMORY VERSES:

Romans 8:1 "There is therefore now no condemnation to those who are in Christ Jesus, who do not walk according to the flesh, but according to the Spirit."

Romans 6:23 "For the wages of sin is death, but the gift of God is eternal life in Christ Jesus, our Lord."

MATTHEW	THEME
40th book of the Bible with 28 chapters	The king and His kingdom of the heavens

For Your Information

FUN FACTS	THE TOP TEN WIDELY SPOKEN LANGUAGES IN THE WORLD	CONGO (DEMOCRATIC REPUBLIC OF THE)
1. Canadian researchers have found that Einstein's brain was 15% wider than the normal brain. 2. Levi Strauss (1829-1902) was an entrepreneur who invented and marketed blue jeans.	1) Mandarin-Chinese 2) English 3) Hindustani 4) Spanish 5) Russian 6) Arabic 7) Bengali 8) Portuguese 9) Malay-Indonesia 10) French	...is in the continent of Africa; Kinshasa is the capital. DR Congo is the 2nd largest country in Africa and the 11th largest by land mass in the world. The Republic is the 19th most populous nation in the world, the 4th most populous nation in Africa, as well as the most populous official Francophone country.

GROUP DISCUSSION AND CLOSING PRAYER

"What it's like to be a parent: It's one of the hardest things you'll ever do but in exchange it teaches you the meaning of unconditional love."

Nicholas Sparks

Day 47 ~ Moses' First Encounter with Pharaoh

OPENING PRAYER
READ: Exodus 5:1-19

Afterward Moses and Aaron...

1) What was Pharaoh's response when Moses and Aaron appeared before him? _____
_____
_____

2) What comments did the king say to his taskmasters and officials about the people of Israel? _____
_____

3) What was the result when Pharaoh said "You are idle! Idle!"? _____
_____

Explore God's World

MEMORY VERSES:

Romans 8:1 "There is therefore now no condemnation to those who are in Christ Jesus, who do not walk according to the flesh, but according to the Spirit."

Romans 6:23 "For the wages of sin is death, but the gift of God is eternal life in Christ Jesus, our Lord."

MARK	THEME
41st book of the Bible with 16 chapters	The service and sacrifice of the servant

For Your Information

FUN FACTS	THE TOP TEN WIDELY SPOKEN LANGUAGES IN THE WORLD	COSTA RICA
1. One recycled glass bottle would save enough energy to power a computer for about 25 minutes. 2. Beethoven had a ritual before composing. He liked to dip his head in cold water before getting creative.	1) Mandarin-Chinese 2) English 3) Hindustani 4) Spanish 5) Russian 6) Arabic 7) Bengali 8) Portuguese 9) Malay-Indonesia 10) French	...is in the continent of North America; San Jose is the capital. In 2012, Costa Rica became the first country in the Americas to ban recreational hunting. The country is famous for its gourmet coffee beans, as well as for its beautiful beaches and mountainside.

GROUP DISCUSSION AND CLOSING PRAYER

"Life, for a child of God, isn't about your successes or failures; Christ is your success."

Jenari Skye

Day 48 ~ The Aftermath of the Encounter

Then the Lord said...

OPENING PRAYER
READ: Exodus 6:1-13

1) What did God say to Moses in verses 2 and 11? _____
_____
_____

2) What was Moses excuse to the Lord? _____
_____

3) What was God's command for Pharaoh? _____
_____

Explore God's World

MEMORY VERSES:
Romans 8:1 "There is therefore now no condemnation to those who are in Christ Jesus, who do not walk according to the flesh, but according to the Spirit."
Romans 6:23 "For the wages of sin is death, but the gift of God is eternal life in Christ Jesus, our Lord."

LUKE	THEME
42nd book of the Bible with 24 chapters	The authority of the Son of Man

For Your Information

FUN FACTS	THE TOP TEN WIDELY SPOKEN LANGUAGES IN THE WORLD	COTE D'IVOIRE (IVORY COAST)
1. Earth is the only planet not named after a Roman god or goddess. 2. While yellow is considered a cheerful color, people are more likely to lose their tempers in yellow rooms and babies tend to cry more.	1) Mandarin-Chinese 2) English 3) Hindustani 4) Spanish 5) Russian 6) Arabic 7) Bengali 8) Portuguese 9) Malay-Indonesia 10) French	...is in the continent of Africa; Yamoussoukro is the capital. This country is the top cocoa producer in the world. In recent times, palm oil and bananas are its main sources of revenue. Cote d'Ivoire borders Liberia, Guinea, Mali, Burkina Faso, and Ghana.

GROUP DISCUSSION AND CLOSING PRAYER

"You educate a man; you educate a man. You educate a woman; you educate a generation."

Brigham Young

Day 49 ~ Week in Review

MEMORIZE AND WRITE

Romans 8:1 _____

_____

_____

Romans 6:23 _____

_____

_____

WRITE THE THEME OF THE FOLLOWING BOOKS

a. Haggai _____

b. Zechariah _____

c. Malachi _____

d. Matthew _____

e. Mark _____

f. Luke _____

TRUE OR FALSE — Circle T for true or F for false

T or F   Bogota is the capital of Colombia.

T or F   Zechariah is the 38th book of the Bible with 19 chapters.

T or F   Spanish is the 5th most widely spoken language in the world.

T or F   Comoros is one of the richest countries in Africa.

T or F   The Hindustani language is spoken in India.

T or F   Congo is famous for its cobalt ore, copper and diamonds.

T or F   The theme of Malachi is "Israel against Yahweh."

T or F   Cote d'Ivoire is famous for its gourmet coffee beans.

T or F   The theme of Mark is "Rebuilding the temple before blessing."

T or F   Arabic and Bengali use the same alphabets for writing.

WRITE THE TOP TEN WIDELY SPOKEN LANGUAGES IN THE WORLD_____

_____

_____

_____

FILL IN THE BLANKS

a. Kinshasa is the_____of _____ (Democratic _____of the).

b. Congo is the _____largest producer of_____ore, copper and_____.

c. Matthew's theme the _____ and His_____of the_____.

d. Colombia is _____after_____ and the capital is_____.

e. Canadian_____have found that Einstein's_____was 15%_____than the_____
   brain.

f. Cote d'Ivoire borders_____, Guinea,_____, Burkina_____and_____.

g. Earth is the only_____ not named after a_____god or_____.

h. In 2012, Costa_____became the 1st_____in the _____to ban
   recreational _____.

i. Comoros is the world's _____producer of_____, and a_____ producer of_____.

MATCH THE FOLLOWING

_____ a. Colombia   1. Moroni

_____ b. Congo (Republic of the)   2. Bogota

_____ c. Congo (Democratic Republic of the) 3. San Jose

_____ d. Comoros   4. Yamoussoukro

_____ e. Costa Rica   5. Brazzaville

_____ f. Cote d'Ivoire   6. Kinshasa

IN WHAT WAYS DO WE SEE GOD'S HAND ON MOSES FROM HIS BIRTH THROUGH HIM BECOMING THE LEADER OF THE HEBREW PEOPLE

_____

_____

_____

_____

Bible Word Search

```
U M Z L E J O C F I H A H F R
E G E P G S A A S V T L O H R
C V N A H L U R S R A A R O N
I H D I L A A C E I M U E W V
H B I I R E R T X V R Z B Z U
N K N L L E N A H E E H W A V
U G Z I D U F D O R T C Z I I
S H T E O Q K F J H F O K S B
B E V C H H V I U P A M T D F
S R N N S M F D S S E M P M Z
R E T S A M K S A T S A Y V Z
M I D W I V E S R E R N G F X
X E H Z E H N X S N Q D E H R
N A I D I M A O B T J Y P I J
V K V J P E M K Y E S E U I K
```

AARON	AFTERMATH	CALLING
CHILD	COMMAND	EGYPT
ENCOUNTER	EXCUSE	HOREB
ISRAELITES	LEVI	MIDIAN
MIDWIVES	MOSES	PHARAOH
ROD	SUFFERING	TASKMASTER

Day 50 ~ Second Encounter with Pharaoh & First Plague

OPENING PRAYER
READ: Exodus 7:8-25

Then the Lord...

1) What the wise men, sorcerers, and the Egyptian magicians did against Aaron's rod? _____

_____

_____

2) What did God do to Pharaoh's heart? _____

_____

3) What was the first plague, and how many days did it last?_____

_____

Explore God's World

MEMORY VERSES:

Ephesians 2:8-9 "For by grace you have been saved through faith, and that not of yourselves; it is the gift of God, not of works, lest anyone should boast."

JOHN	THEME
43rd book of the Bible with 21 chapters	Believing in Jesus Christ, the Son of God

For Your Information

FUN FACTS	THE SEVEN RICHEST COUNTRIES IN THE WORLD	CROATIA
1. The mouth of the jellyfish also serves as an anus. 2. Every square inch of skin on the human body has about 32 million bacteria on it. Fortunately, the vast majority of them are harmless.	1) Luxembourg 2) Qatar 3) Norway 4) Switzerland 5) Australia 6) Denmark 7) Sweden	...is in the continent of Europe; Zagreb is the capital. Croatia is famous not only for its maraschino alcohol made with cherries but also for its Dalmatian dogs and the Croatian Moreska (sword dance). The national dress is the craval, a type of necklace worn by men.

GROUP DISCUSSION AND CLOSING PRAYER

"Knowing trees, I understand the meaning of patience. Knowing grass,
I can appreciate persistence."

Hal Borland

Day 51 ~ Frog, Lice, & Flies

OPENING PRAYER
READ: Exodus 8:1-7,16-18, and 20-32

And the Lord spoke...

1) What was the 2nd plague and how did Pharaoh react? _____

_____

_____

2) Describe the 3rd plague? _____

_____

3) What did Moses demand after the 4th plague? _____

_____

Explore God's World

MEMORY VERSES:

Ephesians 2:8-9 "For by grace you have been saved through faith, and that not of yourselves; it is the gift of God, not of works, lest anyone should boast."

ACTS	THEME
44th book of the Bible with 28 chapters	Evangelism

For Your Information

FUN FACTS	THE SEVEN RICHEST COUNTRIES IN THE WORLD	CUBA
Tim Berners-Lee invented the World Wide Web. His first version of the Web was a program named "Enquire," short for "Enquire Within Upon Everything". He wrote the language HTML (hyper text mark-up language) and devised URL's (universal resource locators) to designate the location of each web page. "HTTP" is Hyper Text Transfer Protocol.	1) Luxembourg 2) Qatar 3) Norway 4) Switzerland 5) Australia 6) Denmark 7) Sweden	...is in the continent of North America; Havana is the capital. Christopher Columbus named the country for the town of Cuba, in the district of Beja, in Portugal. Cuban cigars and rum are considered some of the best in the world.

GROUP DISCUSSION AND CLOSING PRAYER

"The most important thing in communication is hearing what isn't said.""

Peter Drucker

Day 52 ~ Cattle, Boils, & Hail

OPENING PRAYER

READ: Exodus 9:1-12 and 22-35

Then the Lord said...

1) What happened to the livestock of the Egyptians and the Israelites? _____
_____
_____

2) When Moses took ashes from a furnace, what did the ashes turned into? _____
_____

3) What was the 7th plague and did Pharaoh's heart soften or harden?_____
_____

Explore God's World

MEMORY VERSES:

Ephesians 2:8-9 "For by grace you have been saved through faith, and that not of yourselves; it is the gift of God, not of works, lest anyone should boast."

ROMANS	THEME
45th book of the Bible with 16 chapters	God's good news about righteousness

For Your Information

FUN FACTS	THE SEVEN RICHEST COUNTRIES IN THE WORLD	CURACAO
1. Younger beavers stay with their parents for the 1st two years of their lives, before being out on their own. 2. Astronauts can increase their height by up to two inches while in space, because of the lack of pressure put on the spine.	1) Luxembourg 2) Qatar 3) Norway 4) Switzerland 5) Australia 6) Denmark 7) Sweden	...is in the continent of North America; Willemstad is the capital. The country is a polyglot society with the official languages of Dutch, Papiamentu, and English. The Shell Oil refinery originated here. Curacao is known for its floating bridge (Queen Emma) that spans 548 feet, across St. Anna Bay, from one side of Willemstad to the other side.

GROUP DISCUSSION AND CLOSING PRAYER

"Yet, God is already there. All the tomorrows of our life have to pass through Him before they can get to us."

F.B. Meyer

Day 53 ~ Locusts & Darkness

OPENING PRAYER
READ: Exodus 10:12-29

Then the Lord said...

1) What was the 8th plague on the Egyptians? _____

_____

_____

2) What happened in verses 16 and 17? _____

_____

3) During the 9th plague, what did Pharaoh say to Moses and Aaron? _____

_____

Explore God's World

MEMORY VERSES:

Ephesians 2:8-9 "For by grace you have been saved through faith, and that not of yourselves; it is the gift of God, not of works, lest anyone should boast."

1ST CORINTHIANS	THEME
46th book of the Bible with 16 chapters	Answers for today's problems from yesterday's church

For Your Information

FUN FACTS	THE SEVEN RICHEST COUNTRIES IN THE WORLD	CYPRUS
1. Central Africa holds the record for the highest twin birthrate, with an average of 27.9 twins per 1,000 births. 2. Cats have scent glands in their paws. When kneading their paws into us, they are marking their territory.	1) Luxembourg 2) Qatar 3) Norway 4) Switzerland 5) Australia 6) Denmark 7) Sweden	...is in the continent of Europe; Nicosia is the capital. Cyprus is the 3rd largest island in the Mediterranean Sea. Greek and Turkish are the two official languages of the country, which is home to some of the oldest water wells in the world. Halloumi cheese originated here.

GROUP DISCUSSION AND CLOSING PRAYER

"Life is not worth living, unless you live it for the One who gave you life."

Anya vonderLuft

Day 54 ~ The 10th Plague & Its Implementation

OPENING PRAYER
READ: Exodus 11:1-10

Then the Lord said...

1) Whom did the plague affect? _____

_____

_____

2) What did the Israelites ask of their neighbors? _____

_____

3) What was Pharaoh's response after this plague? _____

_____

Explore God's World

MEMORY VERSES:

Ephesians 2:8-9 "For by grace you have been saved through faith, and that not of yourselves; it is the gift of God, not of works, lest anyone should boast."

2ND CORINTHIANS	THEME
47th book of the Bible with 13 chapters	Paul's defense of his apostolic ministry

For Your Information

FUN FACTS	THE SEVEN RICHEST COUNTRIES IN THE WORLD	CZECH REPUBLIC
Alfred Bernard Nobel invented many powerful and relatively safe explosives and explosive devices. He left much of his fortune to award prizes (the Nobel prizes) each year to people who made advancements in physics, chemistry, physiology/medicine, literature, and world peace.	1) Luxembourg 2) Qatar 3) Norway 4) Switzerland 5) Australia 6) Denmark 7) Sweden	…is in the continent of Europe; Prague is the capital. This country, with hundreds of castles everywhere, has three leading sports: ice hockey, football, and sport shooting. The Republic has one of the least religious populations in the world.

GROUP DISCUSSION AND CLOSING PRAYER

"A man does not have to be an angel to be a saint."

Albert Schweitzer

Day 55 ~ The Passover & the Beginning of Exodus

Now the Lord spoke...

OPENING PRAYER

READ: Exodus 12:1-11 and 29-51

1) What was the importance of the 10th month among the Israelites? _____
_____
_____

2) How were they instructed to eat the lamb? _____
_____
_____

3) What were the Passover regulations? _____
_____

Explore God's World

MEMORY VERSES:

Ephesians 2:8-9 "For by grace you have been saved through faith, and that not of yourselves; it is the gift of God, not of works, lest anyone should boast."

GALATIANS	THEME
48th book of the Bible with 6 chapters	The law as tutor

For Your Information

FUN FACTS	THE SEVEN RICHEST COUNTRIES IN THE WORLD	DENMARK (KINGDOM OF DENMARK)
1. The 200 plus corpses on Mount Everest are used as identification points for the climbers. 2. By thickening the brain cortex, spirituality and religion can reduce your risk of developing depression anxiety.	1) Luxembourg 2) Qatar 3) Norway 4) Switzerland 5) Australia 6) Denmark 7) Sweden	...is in the continent of Europe; Copenhagen is the capital. This country consists of the peninsula Jutland and the Danish archipelago of 407 islands, of which around 70 are inhabited. Home of the Vikings, Denmark has three official languages: Danish, Faroese and Greenlandic.

GROUP DISCUSSION AND CLOSING PRAYER

"Because I was enabled by God's grace to trust Him, He has always come to my aid. I delight in speaking well of His name."

George Mueller

Day 56 ~ Week in Review

TRUE OR FALSE — Circle T for true or F for false

T or F   Croatia is famous for Dalmatian dogs and the Moreska.

T or F   Norway is the 3rd richest country in the world.

T or F   Cuba is famous for its high peaks in South America.

T or F   Acts is the 44th book of the Bible with 28 chapters.

T or F   Curacao is known for a floating bridge from Willemstad.

T or F   Qatar is one of the poorest nations in Arab world.

T or F   1st Corinthians has 16 chapters.

T or F   Prague is the capital of Cuba.

T or F   Denmark is considered the home of the Vikings.

T or F   Greek and Turkish are the two official languages of Cyprus.

FILL IN THE BLANKS

a. Noble Prize awards include_____, Chemistry, _____/_____, Literature, and_____.

b. Curacao is a_____society with the_____languages of Dutch,_____, and_____.

c. Danish,_____ and _____are the_____languages of _____.

d. The_____leading sports in Czech are_____, football and _____.

e. Cats have scent _____ in their paws. When _____their paws into us, they are _____
their_____.

f. Cyprus is_____to some of the_____water _____in the _____.

g. _____women carrying _____tend to eat_____than those carrying_____.

h. Cuban _____and_____are _____ some of_____ in the world.

i. Comoros is the world's _____producer of_____, and a_____ producer of_____.

MEMORIZE AND WRITE

Ephesians 2:8-9 _____

_____

_____

MATCH THE FOLLOWING

_____ a. Believing in Jesus Christ the Son of God	1. Acts
_____ b. Evangelism	2. 1st Corinthians
_____ c. God's Good News about Righteousness	3. Galatians
_____ d. Answers for Today's Problems from Yesterday's Church	4. John
_____ e. Paul's Defense of His Apostolic Ministry	5. Romans
_____ f. The Law as Tutor	6. 2nd Corinthians

DEFINE

plague: _____

_____

_____

LIST THE SEVEN RICHEST COUNTRIES IN THE WORLD_____

_____

_____

LIST THE PLAGUES PHARAOH AND HIS PEOPLE SUFFERED_____

_____

_____

_____

_____

_____

Note, you may make copies of this page to color if multiple family members in the same household want to color the illustration.

Day 57 ~ The Crossing of the Red Sea

OPENING PRAYER
READ: Exodus 14:5-30

Now the Lord spoke...

1) With what force did Pharaoh pursue the children of Israel? _____
_____

2) Seeing the advancing Egyptians, the children of Israel expressed what to Moses? _____
_____

3) To show God's continuing protection, the Angel of God did what? Afterwards, what happened
   to the Red Sea? _____
_____

Explore God's World

MEMORY VERSES:
  Romans 3:23 "For all have sinned and fall short of
    the glory of God."
  Matthew 5:48 "Therefore you shall be perfect, just
    as your Father in heaven is perfect."

EPHESIANS	THEME
49th book of the Bible with 6 chapters	The wealth and walk of the believer

For Your Information

FUN FACTS	THE SEVEN POOREST COUNTRIES IN THE WORLD	DJIBOUTI
1. Flight numbers are often taken out of use after a crash or a serious incident. 2. A study conducted by the University of Hawaii at Manoa, revealed that shorter men live longer lives than tall men.	1) Haiti 2) Equatorial Guinea 3) Zimbabwe 4) Congo (Democratic Republic) 5) Swaziland 6) Eritrea 7) Madagascar	...is in the continent of Africa; Djibouti is the capital. Located in the Horn of Africa. Djibouti borders Eritrea, Ethiopia, Somalia, the Red Sea and the Gulf of Aden. Arabic and French are the two official languages. The currency is Djiboutian franc.

GROUP DISCUSSION AND CLOSING PRAYER

"God grant that I may never live to be useless!"

John Wesley

Day 58 ~ Bitter Waters at Marah

OPENING PRAYER
READ: Exodus 15:22-27

So Moses brought...

1) What happened in the wilderness of Shur, and what did they find in Marah? _____
_____

2) What lesson can one learn from verse 26? _____
_____

3) What did they find in Elim? _____
_____
_____

Explore God's World

MEMORY VERSES:
Romans 3:23 "For all have sinned and fall short of the glory of God."
Matthew 5:48 "Therefore you shall be perfect, just as your Father in heaven is perfect."

PHILIPPIANS	THEME
50th book of the Bible with 4 chapters	Joy in jail

For Your Information

FUN FACTS	THE SEVEN POOREST COUNTRIES IN THE WORLD	DOMINICAN REPUBLIC
1. There is a town called "Paradise" and a town called "Hell" in Michigan. 2. The first, non-leaking, ballpoint pen was invented in 1935 by the Hungarian brothers Lazlo and Georg Biro. Lazlo was a chemist and Georg was a newspaper editor.	1) Haiti 2) Equatorial Guinea 3) Zimbabwe 4) Congo (Democratic Republic) 5) Swaziland 6) Eritrea 7) Madagascar	...is in the continent of North America; Santo Domingo is the capital. This is the only country in the world with a national flag to feature the image of a Bible. The country is also one of the top ten producers of cocoa in the world. The Dominican peso is the national currency.

GROUP DISCUSSION AND CLOSING PRAYER

"Your inner strength is your outer foundation."
Allan Rufus

Day 59 ~ Provision of Miraculous Food

OPENING PRAYER
READ: Exodus 16:4-31

Then Moses and...

1) What did the Lord provide for the children of Israel? _____
_____

2) How did the Lord provide the bread for the Israelites? _____
_____

3) What can we learn from verse 31? _____
_____
_____

Explore God's World

MEMORY VERSES:
Romans 3:23 "For all have sinned and fall short of the glory of God."
Matthew 5:48 "Therefore you shall be perfect, just as your Father in heaven is perfect."

COLOSSIANS	THEME
51st book of the Bible with 4 chapters	The preeminence of Christ

For Your Information

FUN FACTS	THE SEVEN POOREST COUNTRIES IN THE WORLD	EAST TIMOR (TIMOR-LESTE)
1. If you go to Google and enter "do a barrel roll," the entire page will rotate completely. 2. Mickey Mouse wears gloves so that his hands can be seen when they're in front of his body.	1) Haiti 2) Equatorial Guinea 3) Zimbabwe 4) Congo (Democratic Republic) 5) Swaziland 6) Eritrea 7) Madagascar	...is in the continent of Asia; Dili is the capital. The official languages are Portuguese and Tetum. The country, which exports coffee, sandalwood and marble, is one of only two predominantly Roman Catholic countries in Asia, the other being the Philippines.

GROUP DISCUSSION AND CLOSING PRAYER

"I never did anything worth doing by accident, nor did any of my inventions come by accident; they came by work."

Plato

Day 60 ~ Water from a Rock

OPENING PRAYER
READ: Exodus 17:1-7

Then all the congregation...

1) What was the Israelites' attitude when they had no water? _____

_____

2) What happened when Moses didn't follow God's commands? _____

_____

3) What does verse 7 say about the attitude of Israelites? _____

_____

_____

Explore God's World

MEMORY VERSES:

Romans 3:23 "For all have sinned and fall short of the glory of God."

Matthew 5:48 "Therefore you shall be perfect, just as your Father in heaven is perfect."

1ST THESSALONIANS	THEME
52nd book of the Bible with 5 chapters	Relationship, review, and rapture

For Your Information

FUN FACTS	THE SEVEN POOREST COUNTRIES IN THE WORLD	ECUADOR
1. "Almost" is the longest word in the English language with all the letters in alphabetical order. 2. A glacier in Antarctica is called "Blood Falls" because it regularly pours out red liquid.	1) Haiti 2) Equatorial Guinea 3) Zimbabwe 4) Congo (Democratic Republic) 5) Swaziland 6) Eritrea 7) Madagascar	...is in the continent of South America; Quito is the capital. Spanish is official language and the $US dollar is the currency. If we measure what peak is farthest from the center of the Earth, Mount Chimborazo is actually 1.5 miles (7,000 ft) farther into space than any of the Himalayas. The most popular sport is soccer (football).

GROUP DISCUSSION AND CLOSING PRAYER

"Love is not patronizing and charity isn't about pity, it is about love. Charity and love are the same. With charity you give love, so don't just give money but reach out your hand instead."

Mother Teresa

Day 61 ~ *The Commandments*

OPENING PRAYER
READ: Exodus 20:1-21

And God spoke...

1) How many commandments are there for the children of Israel to follow? _____
_____

2) Which commandment is with the promise? _____
_____

3) What is the importance of the Sabbath? _____
_____
_____

Explore God's World

MEMORY VERSES:
Romans 3:23 "For all have sinned and fall short of the glory of God."
Matthew 5:48 "Therefore you shall be perfect, just as your Father in heaven is perfect."

2ND THESSALONIANS	THEME
53rd book of the Bible with 3 chapters	End-Time encouragement

For Your Information

FUN FACTS	THE SEVEN POOREST COUNTRIES IN THE WORLD	EGYPT
1. In Japan, there are more pets than there are children. 2. Bandages for wounds have been around since ancient times. Earle Dickson perfected the BAND-AID in 1920 by making a small, sterile adhesive bandage for home use.	1) Haiti 2) Equatorial Guinea 3) Zimbabwe 4) Congo (Democratic Republic) 5) Swaziland 6) Eritrea 7) Madagascar	...is in the continent of Africa; Cairo is the capital. Egypt has the longest history of any modern state. The country is home to the Great Pyramid of Giza, and the Nile River in Egypt is the longest river in the world. The country has the largest navy in Africa and the Middle East. The famous Al-Azhar University was founded in 970 or 972 AD by the Fatimids.

GROUP DISCUSSION AND CLOSING PRAYER

"Think of the patience God has had for you and let it resonate to others. If you want a more patient world, let patience be your motto."

Steve Maraboli

Day 62 ~ Israel's Sin of Worshiping a Golden Calf

OPENING PRAYER
READ: Exodus 32:1-24

Now when the people...

1) What did the Israelites do with all the gold, and what do their offerings represent?_____

_____

2) What was Aaron's sin against the Lord? _____

_____

3) Aaron justified his sin against the Lord how? _____

_____

_____

Explore God's World

MEMORY VERSES:
Romans 3:23 "For all have sinned and fall short of the glory of God."
Matthew 5:48 "Therefore you shall be perfect, just as your Father in heaven is perfect."

1ST TIMOTHY	THEME
54th book of the Bible with 6 chapters	Leadership manual

For Your Information

FUN FACTS	THE SEVEN POOREST COUNTRIES IN THE WORLD	EL SALVADOR
1. The volcanic rock known as "pumice" is the only rock that can float in water. 2. Footprints and tire tracks left behind by astronauts on the moon will stay there forever, as there is no wind to blow them away.	1) Haiti 2) Equatorial Guinea 3) Zimbabwe 4) Congo (Democratic Republic) 5) Swaziland 6) Eritrea 7) Madagascar	...is in the continent of North America; San Salvador is the capital. El Salvador is known as the "Land of the Volcanoes," with more than 20 volcanoes in the territory. Today, this is the only Central American country that has no visible African population.

GROUP DISCUSSION AND CLOSING PRAYER

"Celebrate who you are in your deepest heart. Love yourself and the world will love you."

Amy Leigh Mercree

Day 63 ~ Week in Review

MEMORIZE AND WRITE

Romans 3:23 _____

_____

_____

Matthew 5:48 _____

_____

_____

WRITE THE THEME OF THE FOLLOWING BOOKS

a. Ephesians _____

b. Philippians _____

c. Colossians _____

d. 1st Thessalonians _____

e. 2nd Thessalonians _____

f. 1st Timothy _____

TRUE OR FALSE — Circle T for true or F for false

T or F   Djibouti borders Chad, Congo and Haiti.

T or F   Dominican Republic has the image of a Bible on its national flag.

T or F   Philippians has only 4 chapters.

T or F   Allan Rufus said "Your inner strength is your outer foundation."

T or F   Haiti is considered as one of the poorest nations in the world.

T or F   "For all have sinned and fall short of the glory of God."

T or F   East Timor has two official languages, i.e. Malay and Thai.

T or F   Peru extends farther into space than any other country.

T or F   Egypt is very rich in oil and natural resources.

T or F   El Salvador is known as the "Land of the volcanoes."

WRITE THE SEVEN POOREST COUNTRIES IN THE WORLD_____

_____

_____

FILL IN THE BLANKS

a. There is a _____ called _____ and a town called_____ in Michigan.

b. Egypt is_____ to the Great _____ of_____ and the longest _____ in
     the world "_____".

c. If you go to_____ and enter "do a_____ roll", the_____ page will_____
     completely.

d. El_____ is the only Central America_____that has no visible _____
     population today.

e. Flight numbers are often_____out of use after a_____or a_____incident.

f. Ecuador has the closest_____to space. Mount _____is actually 1.5 miles
     "higher" than Mount_____.

g. East Timor exports coffee,_____ , and_____ .

h. Dominican_____is the only national_____in the world to_____the
     image of a Bible.

i. Djibouti borders Eritrea, Ethiopia, _____, the_____ Sea and the_____
     of_____ .

MATCH THE FOLLOWING

_____ a. Djibouti   1. Quito

_____ b. Dominican Republic   2. San Salvador

_____ c. East Timor   3. Cairo

_____ d. AEcuador   4. Santa Domingo

_____ e. Egypt   5. Djibouti

_____ f. El Salvador   6. Dili

WRITE THE 10 COMMANDMENTS_____

_____

_____

_____

_____

Coloring Activity

Note, you may make copies of this page to color if multiple family members in the same household want to color the illustration.

Day 64 ~ Joshua's Responsibility

OPENING PRAYER
READ: Joshua 1:1-9

After the death...

1) Whom was chosen by God after Moses' death? _____

_____

2) What was Moses' successor's calling and responsibility? _____

_____

3) What in verse 8 is important in our lives? _____

_____

_____

Explore God's World

MEMORY VERSES:

1 John 4:8 "He who does not love, does not know God, for God is love."

Exodus 34:7 "Keeping mercy for thousands, forgiving iniquity and transgression and sin, by no means clearing the guilty, visiting the iniquity of the fathers upon the children and the children's children to the third and the fourth generation."

2ND TIMOTHY	THEME
55th book of the Bible with 4 chapters	Taps for a Christian soldier

For Your Information

FUN FACTS	THE SEVEN WONDERS OF THE WORLD	EQUATORIAL GUINEA
1. Although earthquakes can be deadly, most are very small and not even felt by humans. 2. The game of basketball was invented by James Naismith in 1891, so that his students could participate in sports during the winter.	1) The Great Pyramid of Egypt 2) The Taj Mahal of India 3) The Great Wall of China 4) Mount Everest in Tibet and Nepal 5) The Grand Canyon in USA 6) Victoria Falls in Zambia and Zimbabwe 7) The Harbor of Rio de Janerio in Brazil	...is in the continent of Africa; Malabo is the capital. It is the only country in Africa whose "de jure" (by law, legally or rightfully) official language is Spanish. The country has become one of sub-Sahara's largest oil producers. The island's volcanic landscapes are also a beautiful backdrops.

GROUP DISCUSSION AND CLOSING PRAYER

"I resolved never to stop until I had come to the goal and achieved my purpose."

David Livingstone

Day 65 ~ Rahab

OPENING PRAYER
READ: Joshua 2:1-21

Now Joshua the son...

1) Why did Joshua send spies to Jericho and who was Rahab? _____
_____

2) How and why did Rahab disobey the king's orders? _____
_____

3) What was the importance of the scarlet cord? _____
_____
_____

Explore God's World

MEMORY VERSES:

1 John 4:8 "He who does not love, does not know God, for God is love."

Exodus 34:7 "Keeping mercy for thousands, forgiving iniquity and transgression and sin, by no means clearing the guilty, visiting the iniquity of the fathers upon the children and the children's children to the third and the fourth generation."

TITUS	THEME
56th book of the Bible with 3 chapters	Sane living in an insane world

For Your Information

FUN FACTS	THE SEVEN WONDERS OF THE WORLD	ERITREA
1. There are 13 ways to spell the "O" sound in French. 2. Piranhas are cannibal fish. They will attack and eat other piranhas when underfed or during a frenzied state.	1) The Great Pyramid of Egypt 2) The Taj Mahal of India 3) The Great Wall of China 4) Mount Everest in Tibet and Nepal 5) The Grand Canyon in USA 6) Victoria Falls in Zambia and Zimbabwe 7) The Harbor of Rio de Janerio in Brazil	...is in the continent of Africa; Asmara is the capital. The country's Human Rights record is considered poor. According to the BBC, Eritrea is the only African country to have no privately owned news media. Independent news media have been banned since 2001.

GROUP DISCUSSION AND CLOSING PRAYER

"The only thing worse than being blind is having sight, but no vision."

Helen Keller

Day 66 ~ Battle of Jericho

OPENING PRAYER
READ: Joshua 6:1-25

Now Jericho was...

1) What instructions of the Lord was Joshua to follow? _____
_____

2) List all the commands the Lord asked them to follow on the seventh day? _____
_____

3) What happened to Rahab after the Israelites' victory Jericho? _____
_____
_____

Explore God's World

MEMORY VERSES:

1 John 4:8 "He who does not love, does not know God, for God is love."

Exodus 34:7 "Keeping mercy for thousands, forgiving iniquity and transgression and sin, by no means clearing the guilty, visiting the iniquity of the fathers upon the children and the children's children to the third and the fourth generation."

PHILEMON	THEME
57th book of the Bible with 1 chapter	Christian forgiveness

For Your Information

FUN FACTS	THE SEVEN WONDERS OF THE WORLD	ESTONIA
1. Japan's birth rate is so low that more adult diapers are sold than baby diapers. 2. In ancient Egypt servants were smeared with honey in order to attract flies away from the pharaoh.	1) The Great Pyramid of Egypt 2) The Taj Mahal of India 3) The Great Wall of China 4) Mount Everest in Tibet and Nepal 5) The Grand Canyon in USA 6) Victoria Falls in Zambia and Zimbabwe 7) The Harbor of Rio de Janerio in Brazil	...is in the continent of Europe; Tallinn is the capital. Skype software was created here. Kiiking, a new sport, was invented by Ado Kosk. These Finnic people's official language is Estonian. The adult literacy rate is 99.8%.

GROUP DISCUSSION AND CLOSING PRAYER

"Riches don't make a man rich, they only make him busier."

Christopher Columbus

Day 67 ~ Gideon Versus Midianites

OPENING PRAYER
READ: Judges 6:7-35

And it came to pass...

1) Why did children of Israel cry unto the Lord God? _____
_____

2) What happened under the terebinth tree? _____
_____

3) Who destroyed the altar of Baal? _____
_____
_____

Explore God's World

MEMORY VERSES:

1 John 4:8 "He who does not love, does not know God, for God is love."

Exodus 34:7 "Keeping mercy for thousands, forgiving iniquity and transgression and sin, by no means clearing the guilty, visiting the iniquity of the fathers upon the children and the children's children to the third and the fourth generation."

HEBREWS	THEME
58th book of the Bible with 13 chapters	The superiority of the person and work of Christ

For Your Information

FUN FACTS	THE SEVEN WONDERS OF THE WORLD	ETHIOPIA
1. All of the bacteria in the human body collectively weighs about 4 pounds. 2. Alessandro Volta invented the first chemical battery in 1800. Alkaline batteries, which are not acidic, are an improved type of storage battery developed by Thomas Edison.	1) The Great Pyramid of Egypt 2) The Taj Mahal of India 3) The Great Wall of China 4) Mount Everest in Tibet and Nepal 5) The Grand Canyon in USA 6) Victoria Falls in Zambia and Zimbabwe 7) The Harbor of Rio de Janerio in Brazil	...is in the continent of Africa; Addis Ababa is the capital. Queen of Sheba was from this Country which is located in the Horn of Africa. Coffee is the largest export. More than 856 bird species and many different breeds of African dogs are found here. Ethiopia has several local calendars.

GROUP DISCUSSION AND CLOSING PRAYER

"It is simply the lack of God living in their soul, and having the world in their hearts instead."

R. Leighton

Day 68 ~ Gideon's Victory

OPENING PRAYER
READ: Judges 7:1-23

Then Jerubbaal and...

1) Who were Jerubbaal and Gideon? What did the Lord say to Gideon at the well of Harod? _____
_____

2) How many people left and how many men remained to battle the Midianites? _____
_____

3) With what kind of weapons did Gideon and his men fight? _____
_____
_____

Explore God's World

MEMORY VERSES:

1 John 4:8 "He who does not love, does not know God, for God is love."

Exodus 34:7 "Keeping mercy for thousands, forgiving iniquity and transgression and sin, by no means clearing the guilty, visiting the iniquity of the fathers upon the children and the children's children to the third and the fourth generation."

JAMES	THEME
59th book of the Bible with 5 chapters	Applied Christianity

For Your Information

FUN FACTS	THE SEVEN WONDERS OF THE WORLD	FIJI
1. China has secret military-style boot camps for internet addicts. 2. Gideon Sundbach sold the improved fasteners (zippers) to the US Army, who put zippers on soldiers' clothing and gear during World War I.	1) The Great Pyramid of Egypt 2) The Taj Mahal of India 3) The Great Wall of China 4) Mount Everest in Tibet and Nepal 5) The Grand Canyon in USA 6) Victoria Falls in Zambia and Zimbabwe 7) The Harbor of Rio de Janerio in Brazil	...is in the continent of Australia (Oceania); Suva is the capital. The country is an archipelago of more than 332 islands, of which 110 are permanently inhabited, and has more than 500 islets. Fiji is famous for its handicrafts and the tagimoucia flower that only grows there.

GROUP DISCUSSION AND CLOSING PRAYER

"And sure enough, even waiting will end...if you can just wait long enough."

William Faulkner

Day 69 ~ Gideon's Pursuit of the Kings of Midian

OPENING PRAYER
READ: Judges 8:1-32

Now the men of Ephraim...

1) How was the anger of Ephraim's men calmed by Gideon? _____
_____

2) What was Gideon's response to the leaders of Succoth and men of Penuel? _____
_____

3) How many sons did Gideon have? After his death, what was the attitude of Israel towards
their God? _____
_____
_____

Explore God's World

MEMORY VERSES:

1 John 4:8 "He who does not love, does not know God, for God is love."

Exodus 34:7 "Keeping mercy for thousands, forgiving iniquity and transgression and sin, by no means clearing the guilty, visiting the iniquity of the fathers upon the children and the children's children to the third and the fourth generation."

1ST PETER 60th book of the Bible with 5 chapters	**THEME** Christian living

For Your Information

FUN FACTS	THE SEVEN WONDERS OF THE WORLD	FINLAND
1. English has only one word for "love", while Sanskrit has 96. 2. "Strengths" is the longest word in the English language with only one vowel.	1) The Great Pyramid of Egypt 2) The Taj Mahal of India 3) The Great Wall of China 4) Mount Everest in Tibet and Nepal 5) The Grand Canyon in USA 6) Victoria Falls in Zambia and Zimbabwe 7) The Harbor of Rio de Janerio in Brazil	...is in the continent of Europe; Helsinki is the capital. Finnish and Swedish are the official languages. Finland have the best-educated and trained work forces in the world. The country has nearly 200,000 lakes and known to have fantastic water quality.

GROUP DISCUSSION AND CLOSING PRAYER

"Everything is created twice, first in the mind and then in reality."

Robin S. Sharma

Day 70 ~ Week in Review

MATCH THE FOLLOWING

_____ a. Equatorial Guinea   1. Tallinn

_____ b. Eritrea   2. Suva

_____ c. Estonia   3. Addis Ababa

_____ d. Ethiopia   4. Helsinki

_____ e. Fiji   5. Malabo

_____ f. Finland   6. Asmara

WRITE THE THEME OF THE FOLLOWING BOOKS

a. 2nd Timothy _____

b. Titus _____

c. Philemon _____

d. Hebrews _____

e. James _____

f. 1st Peter _____

TRUE OR FALSE — Circle T for true or F for false

T or F   Equatorial Guinea is the only Africa country whose official language is Spanish.

T or F   Asmara is the capital of Eritrea and listed in the continent of Asia.

T or F   2nd Timothy has only 4 chapters.

T or F   Skating was invented by Ado Kosh.

T or F   Queen Sheba was from Ethiopia.

T or F   Fiji consists of 349 islands.

T or F   The Harbor of Rio de Janerio is in Brazil.

T or F   The Taj Mahal is in Pakistan.

T or F   Finland has no fresh water lakes.

T or F   1st Peter's theme is Christian Living.

WRITE THE SEVEN WONDERS OF THE WORLD

_____

_____

_____

_____

FILL IN THE BLANKS

a. Finland has nearly _____ lakes and known to have _____ water _____.

b. Fiji is _____ or the _____ flower that only grows there, and their _____.

c. Although earthquakes can be _____ most are very _____ and not even felt by_____.

d. All of the _____ in the human _____ collectively weighs about 4 _____.

e. Japan's birth_____ is so low that more adult _____ are sold than_____ diapers.

f. There are_____ ways to _____ the "O" sound in _____.

g. They are_____ people with Estonian as their official_____.

h. Eritrea is the only_____ country to have no_____ owned news_____.

i. Equatorial_____ is the country whose de jure official_____ is _____.

MEMORIZE AND WRITE

1 John 4:8 _____

_____

_____

Exodus 34:7_____

_____

_____

LIST SOME OF THE BATTLES THAT ISRAEL WON BECAUSE OF A MIRACLE OF GOD

_____

_____

_____

_____

Note, you may make copies of this page to color if multiple family members in the same household want to color the illustration.

Day 71 ~ Samson

OPENING PRAYER
READ: Judges 13:1-24

Again the children of...

1) What instructions were given to Manoah and his wife at the birth of their son Samson?_____
_____

2) What was the response of the angel of God when Manoah asked his name? _____
_____

3) What was the conversation Manoah and his wife had after seeing the angel of God? _____
_____
_____

Explore God's World

MEMORY VERSES:

John 1:1-2 "In the beginning was the Word, and the Word was with God, and the Word was God. He was in the beginning with God."

2ND PETER	THEME
61st book of the Bible with 3 chapters	Fending off false teachers under judgment

For Your Information

FUN FACTS	THE WORLD'S SEVEN TOP TRADING CURRENCIES WITH THEIR COUNTRIES	FRANCE
1. An individual banana is called a finger. A bunch of bananas is called a hand. 2. The location of the world's tallest tree, "Hyperion", is kept secret from all but a few scientists.	1) United States dollar USD ($) 2) Euro EUR (€) 3) Japanese yen JPY (¥) 4) Pound sterling GBP (£) 5) Australian dollar AUD ($) 6) Swiss franc CHF (Fr) 7) Canadian dollar CAD ($)	...is in the continent of Europe; Paris is the capital. France is highly famous for its forts, castles and renowned museums. The country is mainly recognized for fashion, wine-producers, cuisine and for more than 400 different varieties of cheese.

GROUP DISCUSSION AND CLOSING PRAYER

"I have found it to be true many hundreds of times, and therefore I continually say to myself, 'Put your hope in God.'"

George Mueller

Day 72 ~ Samson & the Philistines

OPENING PRAYER

READ: Judges 14:3-20 and 15:1-6

Then his father...

1) What inspired Samson in Timnah, and how did his parents respond to his desire?_____
_____

2) What was the riddle Samson asked the Philistines to solve in 7 days?_____
_____

3) What did Samson do with the 300 foxes he caught?_____
_____
_____

Explore God's World

MEMORY VERSES:

John 1:1-2 "In the beginning was the Word, and the Word was with God, and the Word was God. He was in the beginning with God."

1ST JOHN	THEME
62nd book of the Bible with 5 chapters	Fellowship

For Your Information

FUN FACTS	THE WORLD'S SEVEN TOP TRADING CURRENCIES WITH THEIR COUNTRIES	GABON
1. There are more vacant houses than homeless people in the United States. 2. Luther Burbank was a plant breeder who developed over 800 new strains of plants, including many popular varieties of Idaho potato, plums, prunes, berries, trees, and flowers.	1) United States dollar USD ($) 2) Euro EUR (€) 3) Japanese yen JPY (¥) 4) Pound sterling GBP (£) 5) Australian dollar AUD ($) 6) Swiss franc CHF (Fr) 7) Canadian dollar CAD ($)	...is in the continent of Africa; Libreville is the capital. The country is famous for its green forests and national rich reserves like gold, uranium, magnesium, petroleum, and iron. Education is compulsory for children ages 6 to 16.

GROUP DISCUSSION AND CLOSING PRAYER

"Darkness cannot drive out darkness: only light can do that.
Hate cannot drive out hate: only love can do that."

Martin Luther King Jr.

Day 73 ~ Samson's Culture & the Last Conquest

OPENING PRAYER
READ: Judges 16:4-31

Afterward it happened...

1) Who was Delilah, and what was her relationship with Samson?_____
_____

2) Why was Delilah persistent in questioning Samson? How did she betray him? _____
_____

3) What happened to Samson, and how did he die with the Philistines?_____
_____
_____

Explore God's World

MEMORY VERSES:

John 1:1-2 "In the beginning was the Word, and the Word was with God, and the Word was God. He was in the beginning with God."

2ND JOHN	THEME
63rd book of the Bible with 1 chapter	Love in truth

For Your Information

FUN FACTS	THE WORLD'S SEVEN TOP TRADING CURRENCIES WITH THEIR COUNTRIES	THE GAMBIA
1. 15% of the air you breathe in a subway station is human skin. 2. Elephants are known to die from broken hearts, especially when they are young and separated from their social groups.	1) United States dollar USD ($) 2) Euro EUR (€) 3) Japanese yen JPY (¥) 4) Pound sterling GBP (£) 5) Australian dollar AUD ($) 6) Swiss franc CHF (Fr) 7) Canadian dollar CAD ($)	...is in the continent of Africa; Banjul is the capital. The Gambia is the smallest country on the continent of Africa; English as the official language. The government has many initiatives championing women's empowerment, including free girls' education.

GROUP DISCUSSION AND CLOSING PRAYER

"We make a living by what we get, but we make a life by what we give."

Winston Churchill

Day 74 ~ Naomi Returns with Ruth & Meets Boaz

OPENING PRAYER
READ: Ruth 1:1-15 and 2:1-12

Now it came to pass...

1) What was Naomi's relationship with Ruth? _____
_____

2) Why did Naomi tell Ruth to go back to her country? _____
_____

3) Who was Boaz? What he tell Ruth in verses 11 and 12? _____
_____
_____

Explore God's World

MEMORY VERSES:
John 1:1-2 "In the beginning was the Word, and the Word was with God, and the Word was God. He was in the beginning with God."

3RD JOHN	THEME
64th book of the Bible with 1 chapter	Christian hospitality

For Your Information

FUN FACTS	THE WORLD'S SEVEN TOP TRADING CURRENCIES WITH THEIR COUNTRIES	GEORGIA
1. The song "Jingle Bell" was written for Thanksgiving. 2. A metal can (or canister) for preserving food was invented in 1810 by a Peter Durand of London, England, while the can opener was invented in 1858 by Ezra J. Warner.	1) United States dollar USD ($) 2) Euro EUR (€) 3) Japanese yen JPY (¥) 4) Pound sterling GBP (£) 5) Australian dollar AUD ($) 6) Swiss franc CHF (Fr) 7) Canadian dollar CAD ($)	...is in the continent of Europe; Tbilisi is the capital. Joseph Stalin was an ethnic Georgian. There are more than 2000 mineral springs and over 12,000 historical and cultural monuments in Georgia. Education is mandatory for all children aged 6-14.

GROUP DISCUSSION AND CLOSING PRAYER

"Anger, resentment and jealousy doesn't change the heart of others-it only changes yours."
Shannon L. Alder

Day 75 ~ Boaz Redeems Ruth

OPENING PRAYER

READ: Ruth 3:1-13 and 4:1-12

Then Naomi her mother-in-law...

1) Why did Ruth wash and perfume herself and wear best clothes? _____
_____

2) What was the conversation took place between Ruth and Boaz? _____
_____

3) What did Boaz say to the elders of the town? _____
_____
_____

Explore God's World

MEMORY VERSES:

John 1:1-2 "In the beginning was the Word, and the Word was with God, and the Word was God. He was in the beginning with God."

JUDE	THEME
65th book of the Bible with 1 chapter	Contending for the faith

For Your Information

FUN FACTS	THE WORLD'S SEVEN TOP TRADING CURRENCIES WITH THEIR COUNTRIES	GERMANY
1. 2.6 million bars of soap are discarded daily by the hotel industry in the U.S. alone. 2. The mechanical cash register was invented in 1879 by James Ritty, an American tavern keeper. He nicknamed his cash register the "Incorruptible Cashier."	1) United States dollar USD ($) 2) Euro EUR (€) 3) Japanese yen JPY (¥) 4) Pound sterling GBP (£) 5) Australian dollar AUD ($) 6) Swiss franc CHF (Fr) 7) Canadian dollar CAD ($)	...is located in the continent of Europe; Berlin is the capital. The Protestant Reformation was started by Martin Luther in 1517 in Wittenberg; Germany. The Christmas tree tradition originated from here. In Germany over 300 different kinds of bread and beer are made.

GROUP DISCUSSION AND CLOSING PRAYER

"Our patience will achieve more than our force."

Edmund Burke

Day 76 ~ Hannah's Vow, Samuel, & the Sons of Eli

OPENING PRAYER

READ: 1 Samuel 1:5-22 and 2:12-25

But to Hannah...

1) Who was Hannah, and what was her vow to the Lord?_____

_____

2) Who was Eli, and what were the sins Eli's sons were committing against the Lord?_____

_____

3) For how long did Hannah intend to leave Samuel at the temple? How often did she visit Samuel, and what did she take to give him?_____

_____

Explore God's World

MEMORY VERSES:

John 1:1-2 "In the beginning was the Word, and the Word was with God, and the Word was God. He was in the beginning with God."

REVELATION	THEME
66th book of the Bible with 22 chapters	The unveiling of Jesus Christ

For Your Information

FUN FACTS	THE WORLD'S SEVEN TOP TRADING CURRENCIES WITH THEIR COUNTRIES	GHANA
1. Pope Francis claims that pets and animals can go to heaven. 2. Night vision goggles are green because the human eye can differentiate more shades of green than any other color.	1) United States dollar USD ($) 2) Euro EUR (€) 3) Japanese yen JPY (¥) 4) Pound sterling GBP (£) 5) Australian dollar AUD ($) 6) Swiss franc CHF (Fr) 7) Canadian dollar CAD ($)	...is in the continent of Africa; Accra is the capital. In 1957 Ghana became the first African nation to declare its independence from European colonization. The largest producer of cocoa beans, the country is famous for gold mines, timber products, and oil reserves.

GROUP DISCUSSION AND CLOSING PRAYER

"Rejection is an opportunity for your selection."

Bernard Branson

Day 77 ~ Week in Review

MEMORIZE AND WRITE

John 1:1-2_____

_____

_____

WRITE THE THEME OF THE FOLLOWING BOOKS

a. 2nd Peter_____

b. 1st John_____

c. 2nd John_____

d. 3rd John_____

e. Jude_____

f. Revelation_____

TRUE OR FALSE — Circle T for true or F for false

T or F   The Japanese Yen and Swiss franc holds the same worth in the international market.

T or F   There are precisely 600 different kinds of cheese found in France.

T or F   Ghana and Germany have the same borders.

T or F   The book of Revelation has only 14 chapters.

T or F   Libreville is the capital of Georgia.

T or F   Joseph Stalin was an ethnic Georgian.

T or F   There are over 300 different kinds of bread and beer found in Germany.

T or F   One can trade anywhere in the world with United States dollar (US$).

WRITE THE SEVEN WORLD HIGHEST TRADING CURRENCIES WITH THEIR COUNTRIES

_____

_____

_____

_____

FILL IN THE BLANKS

a. There are more_____houses than_____people in the_____States.

b. France is highly_____for its forts,_____and renowned_____.

c. Georgia has more than_____mineral_____, over 12,000 historical and_____
   monuments.

d. The_____tree tradition_____from Germany.

e. Gambia is the smallest_____on the continent of_____with_____as the official
   _____.

f. Ghana became the 1st_____nation to declare_____from_____
   colonization.

g. An individual_____is called a_____. A bunch of_____is called a hand.

h. 15% of the air you_____in a_____station is_____skin.

MATCH THE FOLLOWING

_____ a. France   1. Berlin

_____ b. Gabon   2. Accra

_____ c. Gambia   3. Paris

_____ d. Georgia   4. Libreville

_____ e. Germany   5. Banjul

_____ f. Ghana   6. Tbilisi

LIST SOME OF THE POSITIVE SPIRITUAL CHARACTERISTICS OF SAMSON, RUTH, BOAZ, AND HANNAH

_____

_____

_____

_____

WHAT CHOICES LED TO SAMSON LOSING GOD'S DIVINE STRENGTH?

_____

_____

_____

_____

Bible Word Search

```
M J S Q A G U R N F P P P R H
V Q U V X D N B I X C H G E A
V M F V T F Q I Y D I I H M N
T S E U Q N O C N L D A L E N
E L P M E T L R I A L L G E A
N A O M I N P S E I E S E D H
S A M S O N T S L Y A L R E L
C W S C C I E E W M A U G R E
T O J R N X D E U H T R M R G
I V V E O D D E C H E B P X N
E T S F S F L R S Z C A G P A
L Z A O B X Z W K X Z B T H D
D W U E J T T V V H Y F I D K
E U X P M M M K Z O Q X W A A
R M A B T F I S A S C D F G K
```

ANGEL	BOAZ	CONQUEST
DELILAH	ELDER	ELI
FOXES	GLEANING	HANNAH
NAOMI	PHILISTINES	PRAYER
REDEEMER	RIDDLE	RUTH
SAMSON	SAMUEL	TEMPLE
VOW	WHEAT	

Day 78 ~ Samuel's Prophetic Work & Israel's First King

OPENING PRAYER

READ: 1st Samuel 3:1-20 and 8:1-9

Now the boy Samuel...

1) What was Samuel thinking when the Lord was calling him? How did he respond? _____
_____

2) What was the conversation Samuel and the Lord had? _____
_____

3) Describe the character of Samuel's sons and why Israel wanted a king instead of them. _____
_____

Explore God's World

MEMORY VERSES:

John 1:14 "And the Word became flesh and dwelt among us, and we beheld His glory, the glory as of the only begotten of the Father, full of grace and truth."

James 2:19 "You believe that there is one God. You do well. Even the demons believe and tremble."

GENESIS

The author is not identified. Traditionally, the author has always assumed to have been Moses. There is no conclusive reason to deny the Mosaic authorship of Genesis

PURPOSE

Genesis has sometimes been called the "seed plot" of the entire Bible. Most of the major doctrines in the Bible are introduced in "seed" form in this Book. Along with the fall of man, God's promise of salvation and redemption is recorded (Genesis 3:15). The doctrines of creation, imputation of sin, justification, atonement, depravity, wrath, grace, sovereignty, responsibility, and many more are addressed in the book of origins called Genesis.

For Your Information

FUN FACTS	THE TOP TEN MANGO PRODUCING COUNTRIES OF THE WORLD	GREECE
1. Due to extreme cold temperature one can't work in Antarctica unless the wisdom tooth and appendix are removed. 2. There are more living organisms in a teaspoonful of soil than there are people on the planet.	1) India 2) China 3) Thailand 4) Indonesia 5) Pakistan 6) Mexico 7) Brazil 8) Bangladesh 9) Nigeria 10) Philippines	...is in the continent of Europe. Athens is the capital. Greece was the home of the great mathematician, Pythagoras, and the great philosophers, Socrates, Plato, and Aristotle. Greece is the birthplace of democracy, the Olympic Games, Western philosophy, literature, and drama, historiography, political science, major scientific and mathematical principles.

GROUP DISCUSSION AND CLOSING PRAYER

"It is better to be hated for what you are, than to be loved for what you are not."

André Gide

Day 79 ~ Samuel Anoints Saul as King

OPENING PRAYER
READ: 1st Samuel 9:1-2, 10-17, 27 and 10:17-24

There was a man...

1) Whom did Samuel anoint as the first king of Israel and to which did tribe he belong?_____
_____

2) How did Samuel anoint Saul, and who approved of Saul becoming king?_____
_____

3) What were God's Words spoken by Samuel to Israel?_____
_____

Explore God's World

MEMORY VERSES:

John 1:14 "And the Word became flesh and dwelt among us, and we beheld His glory, the glory as of the only begotten of the Father, full of grace and truth."

James 2:19 "You believe that there is one God. You do well. Even the demons believe and tremble."

EXODUS
Moses was the author of Exodus. (Exodus 17:14; 24:4-7; 34:27)

PURPOSE
The word "exodus" means departure. In God's timing, the exodus of the Israelites from Egypt marked the end of a period of oppression for Abraham's descendants (Gen.15:13). It was the beginning of the fulfillment of the covenant promise to Abraham, that his descendants would not only live in the promised land, but would also multiply and become a great nation (Gen.12:1-3,7). The purpose of writing Exodus is to show the rapid growth of Jacob's descendants from Egypt to the establishment of the theocratic nation of Israel in the promised land.

For Your Information

FUN FACTS	THE TOP TEN MANGO PRODUCING COUNTRIES OF THE WORLD	GRENADA
1. Pope Francis claims that pets and animals can go to heaven. 2. Night vision goggles are green because the human eye can differentiate more shades of green than any other color.	1) India 2) China 3) Thailand 4) Indonesia 5) Pakistan 6) Mexico 7) Brazil 8) Bangladesh 9) Nigeria 10) Philippines	...is in the continent of North America, Saint George's is the capital. The official language is English. Known as the "Island of Spice," Grenada is one of the world's largest exporters of mace and nutmeg. Cricket is one of the country's most popular sports.

GROUP DISCUSSION AND CLOSING PRAYER

"Let us sing even when we do not feel like it, for in this way we give wings to heavy feet and turn weariness into strength."

John Henry Jowett

Day 80 ~ Samuel's Farewell

OPENING PRAYER
READ: 1st Samuel 12:1-25

Now Samuel said to...

1) What were Samuel's farewell remarks to the nation of Israel?_____

_____

2) What was the concern of the people of Israel after Samuel's farewell speech?_____

_____

3) What did Samuel tell the Israelites in verses 24 and 25? _____

_____

Explore God's World

MEMORY VERSES:

John 1:14 "And the Word became flesh and dwelt among us, and we beheld His glory, the glory as of the only begotten of the Father, full of grace and truth."

James 2:19 "You believe that there is one God. You do well. Even the demons believe and tremble."

EXODUS
Moses was the author of Leviticus.

PURPOSE
Because the Israelites had been held captive in Egypt for 400 years, the concept of God had been distorted by the polytheistic, pagan Egyptians. The purpose of writing Leviticus is to provide instruction and laws to guide a sinful, yet redeemed, people in their relationship with a holy God. There is an emphasis in Leviticus on the need for personal holiness. Sin must be atoned for through the offering of proper sacrifices (chapters 8-10). Other topics covered in the book are clean/unclean foods, childbirth, and diseases (chapters 11-15). Chapter 16 describes the Day of Atonement, when the annual sacrifice is made for the cumulative sins of the people. Likewise, the people of God are to be circumspect in their personal, moral, and social living in contrast to the practices of the heathens around them (Chapters 17-22).

For Your Information

FUN FACTS	THE TOP TEN MANGO PRODUCING COUNTRIES OF THE WORLD	GUATEMALA
1. The smell of chocolate increases theta brain waves, which can help trigger relaxation. 2. African elephants have a special alarm when they come across a beehive and various other threats.	1) India 2) China 3) Thailand 4) Indonesia 5) Pakistan 6) Mexico 7) Brazil 8) Bangladesh 9) Nigeria 10) Philippines	...is in the continent of North America. Guatemala City is the capital. The country is famous for its coffee, which is one of the best in the world, and also for its handicrafts. Spanish is the official language, which is not universally spoken among the indigenous population.

GROUP DISCUSSION AND CLOSING PRAYER

"Love is that condition in which the happiness of another person is essential to your own."

Robert A. Heinlein

Day 81 ~ Rejection of Saul

OPENING PRAYER

READ: 1st Samuel 13:1-13 and 15:10-31

Saul reigned one...

1) Did Saul keep God's command? _____

_____

2) What did Samuel say to Saul about not keeping God's command? _____

_____

3) What did Saul do with the Agag, king of Amalek? _____

_____

Explore God's World

MEMORY VERSES:

John 1:14 "And the Word became flesh and dwelt among us, and we beheld His glory, the glory as of the only begotten of the Father, full of grace and truth."

James 2:19 "You believe that there is one God. You do well. Even the demons believe and tremble."

NUMBERS

Moses was the author of Numbers.

PURPOSE

The message of the book of Numbers is universal and timeless. It reminds believers of the spiritual warfare in which they are engaged, for Numbers is the service and walk of God's people. It essentially bridges the gap between the Israelites receiving the law (Exodus and Leviticus) and preparing them to enter the promised land. (Deuteronomy and Joshua)

For Your Information

FUN FACTS	THE TOP TEN MANGO PRODUCING COUNTRIES OF THE WORLD	GUINEA-BISSAU
1. Crabs can live as long as they keep their gills moist. 2. The first automatic analog cellular phone was made in the 1960's. Commercial models were introduced in Japan by NTT.	1) India 2) China 3) Thailand 4) Indonesia 5) Pakistan 6) Mexico 7) Brazil 8) Bangladesh 9) Nigeria 10) Philippines	...is in the continent of Africa. Bissau is the capital. Only 14% speaks Portuguese while 44% speaks Crioulo, a Portuguese-based Creole language. Education is compulsory from the age of 7 to 13. Islam is practiced by 50% of people.

GROUP DISCUSSION AND CLOSING PRAYER

"The soul hardly ever realizes it, but whether he is a believer or not, his loneliness is really a homesickness for God."

Hubert Van Zeller

Day 82 ~ David's Anointing

OPENING PRAYER

READ: 1st Samuel 16:1-23

Now the LORD...

1) What did the Lord tell Samuel about choosing the new king of Israel?_____
_____

2) Which son of Jesse did the Lord choose? _____
_____

3) Whose help did Saul seek to calm the distressing spirit that tormented him?_____
_____

Explore God's World

MEMORY VERSES:

John 1:14 "And the Word became flesh and dwelt among us, and we beheld His glory, the glory as of the only begotten of the Father, full of grace and truth."

James 2:19 "You believe that there is one God. You do well. Even the demons believe and tremble."

DEUTERONOMY

Moses was the author of Deuteronomy. It's a collection of his sermons to Israel just before they crossed the Jordan. "These are the words which Moses spoke" (Deut.1:1). Someone else (Joshua, perhaps) may have written the last chapter.

PURPOSE

The new generation of Israelites about to enter the promised land had not experienced the miracle at the Red Sea, nor were they present at the giving of the law at Sinai. They were about to enter a new land with many dangers and temptations. Deuteronomy was given to remind them of God's law and God's power.

For Your Information

FUN FACTS	THE TOP TEN MANGO PRODUCING COUNTRIES OF THE WORLD	GUYANA
1. In the early Renaissance period, many plastic surgeries were performed in barber shops. 2. A woman who survived a plane explosion in 1972 was awarded the Guinness Record title for the highest fall without a parachute at 33,000 feet.	1) India 2) China 3) Thailand 4) Indonesia 5) Pakistan 6) Mexico 7) Brazil 8) Bangladesh 9) Nigeria 10) Philippines	...is in the continent of South America. Georgetown is the capital. Guyana is an Amerindian word meaning "land of many waters." There are nine indigenous tribes. The two largest groups are the Indo-Guyanese (East Indians) and the Afro-Guyanese. The major sports in Guyana is cricket. The currency is Guyanese dollar (GYD).

GROUP DISCUSSION AND CLOSING PRAYER

"Challenge yourself with something you know you could never do, and what you'll find is that you can overcome anything."

Anonymous

Day 83 ~ David's Victory Over Goliath

And a champion went...

OPENING PRAYER
READ: 1st Samuel 17:4-51

1) Describe the appearance of Goliath._____
_____

2) Who responded to Goliath's Challenge? _____

3) What weapons did David use to defeat Goliath?_____

Explore God's World

MEMORY VERSES:

John 1:14 "And the Word became flesh and dwelt among us, and we beheld His glory, the glory as of the only begotten of the Father, full of grace and truth."

James 2:19 "You believe that there is one God. You do well. Even the demons believe and tremble."

JOSHUA

The book does not explicitly name its author. More than likely, Joshua the son of Nun, and the successor of Moses as leader over Israel, penned much of this book. The latter part was written by at least one other person, after the death of Joshua. It is also possible that several sections were edited/compiled following Joshua's death.

PURPOSE

Joshua provides an overview of the military campaigns to conquer the land area that God had promised. Following the exodus from Egypt and the subsequent forty years of the wilderness wanderings, the newly-formed nation is now poised to enter the promised land, conquer the inhabitants, and occupy the territory. This overview gives abbreviated and selective details of many of the battles and the manner in which the land was not only conquered, but also how it was divided into tribal areas.

For Your Information

FUN FACTS	THE TOP TEN MANGO PRODUCING COUNTRIES OF THE WORLD	HAITI
1. Charles Darwin and Abraham Lincoln were born on the same day, February 12, 1809. 2. In the Caribbean Islands and other parts of the world, donkey and horse meat are common ingredients in pepperoni.	1) India 2) China 3) Thailand 4) Indonesia 5) Pakistan 6) Mexico 7) Brazil 8) Bangladesh 9) Nigeria 10) Philippines	...is in the continent of North America. Port-au-Prince is the capital. Discovered in 1492 by Christopher Columbus, Haiti is the poorest country in the Western Hemisphere. Three quarters of the population live on US $ 2.00 or less per day. The country exports crops such as mangoes, cacao, and coffee.

GROUP DISCUSSION AND CLOSING PRAYER

"The measure of a Christian is not in the height of his grasp, but in the depth of his love."

Clarence Jordan

Day 84 ~ Week in Review

MATCH THE FOLLOWING

_____ a. Genesis	1. Georgetown
_____ b. Greece	2. Port-au-Prince
_____ c. Exodus	3. Saint George
_____ d. Grenada	4. Guatemala City
_____ e. Guatemala	5. Military Campaigns
_____ f. Haiti	6. India
_____ g. Guinea-Bissau	7. Bissau
_____ h. Numbers	8. Unknown
_____ i. Guyana	9. Moses
_____ j. Mangoes	10. Athens
_____ k. Joshua	11. Moses

TRUE OR FALSE — Circle T for true or F for false

T or F   You believe that there is one God. You do well. Even the demons believe and tremble.

T or F   Guatemala is in the continent of Asia.

T or F   The official language of Grenada is English.

T or F   Genesis, Leviticus, and Numbers were written by Moses.

T or F   Numbers is the book of the service and the walk of God's people.

T or F   The word "Exodus" means departure.

T or F   14% of the Guinea-Bissau population speak Portuguese.

T or F   The major sport in Guyana is martial arts.

T or F   Leviticus' purpose is to relate the life of Joshua.

T or F   Democracy originated from Greece.

T or F   Haiti was discovered by the a French explorer.

LIST THE TOP TEN MANGO PRODUCING COUNTRIES OF THE WORLD

_____

_____

FILL IN THE BLANKS

a. The_____ of the_____of Numbers is_____and timeless.

b. The two_____groups are the Indo-_____(East Indians) and the_____-Guyanese.

c. You_____work in Antarctica unless your_____teeth and_____are removed.

d. Grenada is one of the_____largest_____of mace and_____.

e. The_____of Deuteronomy was given to_____them of_____ law and God's_____.

f. Guatemala is_____for its_____which is one of the_____ in the_____.

g. Pope_____claims that_____and_____can_____to heaven.

h. Greece is_____of Pythagoras, the great_____, and Socrates,_____,
   Aristotle the great_____.

i. Genesis has_____ been called the "_____-plot" of the_____Bible.

j. "It is better to be_____ for what you_____than to be_____for what you are
   _____."

k. It is also_____that several_____were edited /_____following Joshua's_____.

MEMORIZE AND WRITE

John 1:14 _____

_____

_____

James 2:19_____

_____

_____

DESCRIBE HOW GOD INITIALLY CALLED SAMUEL. THEN LIST SOME WAYS GOD USED SAMUEL IN THE LIVES OF SAUL AND DAVID.

_____

_____

_____

_____

_____

David & Goliath Coloring Activity

Note, you may make copies of this page to color if multiple family members in the same household want to color the illustration.

Day 85 ~ Saul's Punitive Action Against the Priests of Nob

OPENING PRAYER
READ: 1st Samuel 22:1-23

David therefore departed...

1) What did Doeg tell Saul?_____

_____

2) What were Saul's actions after calling for the priests of Nob?_____

_____

3) Who escaped and told David about the killing of the priests?_____

_____

Explore God's World

MEMORY VERSES:

Isaiah 53:6 "All we like sheep have gone astray; we have turned, every one, to his own way; and the Lord has laid on Him the iniquity of us all."

Isaiah 40:11 "He will feed His flock like a shepherd; He will gather the lambs with His arm, and carry them in His bosom, and gently lead those who are with young."

JUDGES

The book does not specifically name its author. The tradition holds that Samuel was the author. Internal evidence indicates that the author lived shortly after the period of the Judges. Therefore, Samuel fits this qualification.

PURPOSE

Judges can be divided into two sections: 1) Chapters 1-16 give an account of the wars of deliverance beginning with the Israelites' defeat of the Canaanites, and ending with the defeat of the Philistines and the death of Samson. 2) Chapters 17-21 are an appendix and do not relate to the previous chapters. These chapters are noted as a time "when there was no king in Israel" (Judges 17:6; 18:1; 19:1; 21:25). Ruth was originally a part of Judges, but in A.D. 450 it was removed to become a book of its own.

For Your Information

FUN FACTS	TEN COUNTRIES WITH THE HIGHEST DEFORESTATION	HONDURAS
1. The only domestic animal which is not mentioned in the Bible is the cat. 2. The Pineapple is not a single fruit, but a group of berries fused together.	1) Brazil 2) Indonesia 3) Russian Federation 4) Mexico 5) Papua New Guinea 6) Peru 7) USA 8) Bolivia 9) Sudan 10) Nigeria	...is in the continent of North America; Tegucigalpa is the capital. Honduras, which literally means "depths" in Spanish, was at times referred to as Spanish Honduras to differentiate it from British Honduras, which became the modern-day state of Belize.

GROUP DISCUSSION AND CLOSING PRAYER

"Love looks not with the eyes, but with the mind, and therefore is winged Cupid painted blind."

William Shakespeare

Day 86 ~ Saul's Pursuit of David in the Wilderness

OPENING PRAYER

READ: 1st Samuel 23:6-14 and 24:1-22

Now it happened...

1) Who told Saul about David's location?_____

_____

2) Why did David spare Saul's life? _____

_____

3) What oath did Saul ask of David after sparing Saul's life?_____

_____

Explore God's World

MEMORY VERSES:

Isaiah 53:6 "All we like sheep have gone astray; we have turned, every one, to his own way; and the Lord has laid on Him the iniquity of us all."

Isaiah 40:11 "He will feed His flock like a shepherd; He will gather the lambs with His arm, and carry them in His bosom, and gently lead those who are with young."

RUTH

The book does not specifically name its author. The tradition is that prophet Samuel wrote Ruth.

PURPOSE

Ruth is written to the Israelites. It teaches that genuine love at times may require uncompromising sacrifice. Regardless of our lot in life, we can live according to the precepts of God. Genuine love and kindness will be rewarded. God abundantly blesses those who seek to live obedient lives. Obedient living does not allow for "accidents" in God's plan. God extends mercy to the merciful.

For Your Information

FUN FACTS	TEN COUNTRIES WITH THE HIGHEST DEFORESTATION	HUNGARY
1. The place where military personnel socialize and eat is called the mess hall. 2. African-American men were not deemed equal members of the Mormon Church until 1978.	1) Brazil 2) Indonesia 3) Russian Federation 4) Mexico 5) Papua New Guinea 6) Peru 7) USA 8) Bolivia 9) Sudan 10) Nigeria	...is in the continent of Europe. Budapest is the capital. The country is most famous for its world renowned spas and thermal bath spots. The first Bible translation was completed in 1439. Hungary is home to the world's largest thermal water cave system. Their currency is Forint and the national sports is football.

GROUP DISCUSSION AND CLOSING PRAYER

"Let us sing God's praises in anticipation of things to come."

Charles H. Spurgeon

Day 87 ~ Samuel's Death & David's Marriage

OPENING PRAYER

READ: 1st Samuel 25:1, 18-43

Then Samuel died...

1) What message did David give his men to deliver to Nabal?_____
_____

2) Describe what it means to stop "avenging myself with my own hand"? (verse 33)_____
_____

3) Who was Abigail and what happened to her after Nabal's death?_____
_____

Explore God's World

MEMORY VERSES:

Isaiah 53:6 "All we like sheep have gone astray; we have turned, every one, to his own way; and the Lord has laid on Him the iniquity of us all."

Isaiah 40:11 "He will feed His flock like a shepherd; He will gather the lambs with His arm, and carry them in His bosom, and gently lead those who are with young."

1ST SAMUEL

The author of the book is anonymous. We know that Samuel wrote 1st Samuel 10:25, and it is very possible that he wrote other parts of this book as well. Other possible contributors to 1st Samuel are the prophets/historians Nathan and Gad. (1st Chronicles 29:29)

PURPOSE

1st Samuel records the history of Israel in the land of Canaan as they move from the rule of judges to being a unified nation under kings. Samuel emerges as the last judge and he anoints the first two kings, Saul and David.

For Your Information

FUN FACTS	TEN COUNTRIES WITH THE HIGHEST DEFORESTATION	ICELAND
1. There is a city in Turkey called "Batman." 2. Dr. John S. Pemberton (1830-1888) who invented Coca-Cola on May 8th,1886 in Atlanta, GA, invented many syrups, medicines, and elixirs.	1) Brazil 2) Indonesia 3) Russian Federation 4) Mexico 5) Papua New Guinea 6) Peru 7) USA 8) Bolivia 9) Sudan 10) Nigeria	...is in the continent of Europe. Reykjavik is the capital. Iceland has many hot springs, geysers and volcanoes and is the only country with no standing army. The country has a high level of car ownership per capita, with a car for every 1.5 inhabitants.

GROUP DISCUSSION AND CLOSING PRAYER

"Patience is not passive waiting. Patience is active acceptance of the process required to attain your goals and dreams."

Ray Davis

Day 88 ~ Again Saul Pursues David in the Wilderness

OPENING PRAYER
READ: 1st Samuel 26:1-25

Now the Ziphites...

1) Where did Saul and his men camp? _____
_____

2) Who went with David to Saul's camp? _____
_____

3) What did David take from Saul? _____
_____

Explore God's World

MEMORY VERSES:

Isaiah 53:6 "All we like sheep have gone astray; we have turned, every one, to his own way; and the Lord has laid on Him the iniquity of us all."

Isaiah 40:11 "He will feed His flock like a shepherd; He will gather the lambs with His arm, and carry them in His bosom, and gently lead those who are with young."

2ND SAMUEL
The book does not identify its author. It could not be the prophet Samuel, since he died in 1st Samuel. Possible writers include Nathan and Gad (1st Chronicles 29:29).
PURPOSE
2nd Samuel records King David's reign. It places the Davidic Covenant in its historical context.

For Your Information

FUN FACTS	TEN COUNTRIES WITH THE HIGHEST DEFORESTATION	INDIA
1. "Nomophobia" is the fear of being without a cell phone or being without mobile phone contact. 2. The colors yellow and orange are not recommended for use in kitchens as they are known to be appetite stimulators.	1) Brazil 2) Indonesia 3) Russian Federation 4) Mexico 5) Papua New Guinea 6) Peru 7) USA 8) Bolivia 9) Sudan 10) Nigeria	...is in the continent of Asia. New Delhi is the capital. The country is the largest democracy in the world. Famous monuments in India are the Taj Mahal, Khajuraho and its temples, which are said to be weighted with gold.

GROUP DISCUSSION AND CLOSING PRAYER

**"Just when you think it can't get any worse, it can;
and just when you think it can't get any better, it can."**

Nicholas Sparks

Helping Parents Develop Their Children's Love for God and for People

111

Day 89 ~ People of Ziklag & the Amalekites

OPENING PRAYER
READ: 1st Samuel 30:1-26

Now it happened...

1) What did the Amalekites do after raiding Negev and Ziklag?_____
_____

2) Who led David and his men to the Amalekites?_____
_____

3) Where did David send some of the spoil?_____
_____

Explore God's World

MEMORY VERSES:

Isaiah 53:6 "All we like sheep have gone astray; we have turned, every one, to his own way; and the Lord has laid on Him the iniquity of us all."

Isaiah 40:11 "He will feed His flock like a shepherd; He will gather the lambs with His arm, and carry them in His bosom, and gently lead those who are with young."

1ST KINGS

The book does not specifically name its author. Traditionally, it is thought to be written by the prophet, Jeremiah.

PURPOSE

1st Kings is the sequel to 1st and 2nd Samuel and begins by tracing Solomon's rise to kingship after the death of David. The story begins with a united kingdom, but ends in a nation divided into two kingdoms, known as Judah and Israel.

For Your Information

FUN FACTS

1. One in every 2,000 babies is born with a tooth.
2. Ruth Wakefield invented chocolate chips (and cookies) in 1930. Her new cookie invention was and still is called the "Toll House Cookie."

TEN COUNTRIES WITH THE HIGHEST DEFORESTATION

1) Brazil 2) Indonesia
3) Russian Federation 4) Mexico
5) Papua New Guinea 6) Peru
7) USA 8) Bolivia 9) Sudan
10) Nigeria

INDONESIA

...is in the continent of Asia. Jakarta is the capital. The country consists of 18,110 islands, which makes it the largest archipelago and it has the 2nd largest tropical rain forest in the world. Mountain Krakatoa is one of the most active volcanoes in the world.

GROUP DISCUSSION AND CLOSING PRAYER

"How can you expect to dwell with God forever, if you so neglect and forsake Him here?"

Jonathan Edwards

Day 90 ~ Death of Saul

OPENING PRAYER
READ: 1st Samuel 31:1-13

Now the Philistines...

1) What did Saul say to his armor-bearer?_____

_____

2) How did Saul die?_____

_____

3) What did the Philistines do after they found the bodies of Saul and three of his sons?_____

_____

Explore God's World

MEMORY VERSES:

Isaiah 53:6 "All we like sheep have gone astray; we have turned, every one, to his own way; and the Lord has laid on Him the iniquity of us all."

Isaiah 40:11 "He will feed His flock like a shepherd; He will gather the lambs with His arm, and carry them in His bosom, and gently lead those who are with young."

2ND KINGS

The book does not name its author. Traditionally Jeremiah was the author of both 1st and 2nd Kings.

PURPOSE

2nd Kings is a sequel of 1st Kings and continues the story of the kings of the divided kingdoms (Israel and Judah). 2nd Kings concludes with the final overthrow and deportation of the people of Israel and Judah to Assyria and Babylon, respectively. 1st and 2nd Kings are combined into one book in the Hebrew Bible.

For Your Information

FUN FACTS	TEN COUNTRIES WITH THE HIGHEST DEFORESTATION	IRAN
1. Every time you form a memory, new brain connections are created. 2. Residents of Churchill, Canada leave their cars unlocked to offer an escape for pedestrians who might encounter a Polar bear.	1) Brazil 2) Indonesia 3) Russian Federation 4) Mexico 5) Papua New Guinea 6) Peru 7) USA 8) Bolivia 9) Sudan 10) Nigeria	...is in the continent of Asia. Tehran is the capital. Home to one of the world's oldest civilizations, Iran has the largest proven gas reserves in the world and also ranks 3rd in oil reserves. Iran is the birthplace of free-style wrestling and polo.

GROUP DISCUSSION AND CLOSING PRAYER

"Knowing trees, I came to realize, understand and appreciate the act of patience."

Ogwo David Emenike

Day 91 ~ Week in Review

MEMORIZE AND WRITE

Isaiah 53:6 _____

_____

_____

Isaiah 40:11 _____

_____

_____

TRUE OR FALSE — Circle T for true or F for false

T or F   Mount Krakatoa is one of the most active volcanoes in the world.

T or F   The authors of 1st and 2nd Kings were the kings and rulers of that time.

T or F   India has the largest democracy in the world.

T or F   The Book of Ruth was written to the Israelites.

T or F   Iran is the birth place of freestyle wrestling and polo.

T or F   The Book of Judges does not specifically name the author.

T or F   Patience is not a virtue. It is an achievement.

T or F   Iceland is the only country with no standing army.

T or F   The 1st Bible translation was completed in Hungary in 1439.

T or F   Honduras literally means "depths" in Spanish.

T or F   Saudi Arabia and Sudan are two of the highest deforestation countries.

MATCH THE FOLLOWING

_____ a. Iran   1. Highest Deforestation

_____ b. Indonesia   2. Prophet Jeremiah

_____ c. India   3. Samuel

_____ d. Iceland   4. Jakarta

_____ e. Honduras   5. Tehran

_____ f. Hungary   6. Honduras

_____ g. 1st & 2nd Kings   7. New Delhi

_____ h. Brazil   8. Budapest

_____ i. British   9. Reykjavik

_____ j. Ruth   10. Tegucigalpa

LIST TEN COUNTRIES WITH THE HIGHEST DEFORESTATION

_____

_____

_____

_____

FILL IN THE BLANKS

a. Hungry is_____to the largest _____water_____system.

b. Indonesia consists of_____islands which makes it the largest_____and the 2nd largest tropical rain forest in the world.

c. Iceland has a_____level of_____ownership per capita; with a car for every 1.5_____.

d. Honduras, which_____means "_____" in _____.

e. Every_____you form a_____, new brain _____are created.

f. Ruth_____that_____love at times may_____uncompromising sacrifice.

g. The only domestic_____which is not _____ in the Bible is the_____.

h. Nomophobia is the_____of being without a_____or being_____ mobile phone contact.

i. 1st and 2nd Kings are _____into one book in the Hebrew_____.

j. Iran has the_____proven gas_____ in the world and_____ ranks_____in oil reserves.

DESCRIBE THE RELATIONSHIP OF SAUL AND DAVID

_____

_____

_____

_____

Note, you may make copies of this page to color if multiple family members in the same household want to color the illustration.

Glossary & References

A

Abbreviated—[uh-bree-vee-ey-tid] To shorten or reduce (anything) in length.

Aboriginal—[ab-uh-rij-uh-nl] Original or earliest known; native; indigenous.

Accumulation—[uh-kyoo-myuh-ley-shuh n] Something that has been collected, gathered.

Admonished—[ad-mon-ish] To caution, advise, or counsel against something.

Ancient—Dating from a remote period; of great age.

Adulterous—Unfaithful

Alleviate—[uh-lee-vee-eyt] lighten, easier to bear, relieve.

Anonymous—uh-non-uh-muh s] Without any name acknowledged, as that of author or Contributor.

Apocalyptic—[uh-pok-uh-lip-tik] Predicting an imminent disaster or universal destruction.

Apokalupsis—[uh-pok-uh-lips] Any revelation or prophecy.

Apostolic—[ap-uh-stol-ik] Pertaining to or characteristic of the 12 Apostles.

Archipelago—[ahr-kuh-pel-uh-goh] Any large body of water with many islands.

Asceticism—[uh-set-uh-siz uh m] The doctrine that a person can attain a high spiritual and moral state by practicing self-denial, self-mortification, and the like.

Asymmetrical—[ey-suh-me-trik, as-uh-] not identical on both sides of a central line, unsymmetrical.

Atonement—The reconciliation of man with God through the life, sufferings, and sacrificial death of Jesus Christ

Atrocities—[uh-tros-i-tee] Behaviour or an action that is wicked or ruthless.

Autobiographical—Marked by or dealing with one's own experiences or life history.

Autopsy—[aw-top-see] inspection of a body after death, as for determination of the cause of death.

B

Beethoven—German composer (1770–1827)

Beetle—Any of various insects resembling the beetle, as a cockroach.

Bosom—The breast of a human being.

Botany—The branch of biology that deals with plant life.

C

Camouflage—[kam-uh-flahzh] As by painting or screening objects so that they are lost lost to view in thebackground.

Cannibals—Any animal that eats its own kind.

Cays—A small low Island

Cerinthianism—A heresy taught that deals with the person of Jesus.

Cessation—[se-sey-shuh n] a temporary or complete stopping; discontinuance.

Chronicles—A record or register of events in chronological order

Chronological—A sequence of events, arranged in order of occurrence.

Circumcision—The rite of circumcising, spiritual purification.

Circumspect—[sur-*kuh* m-spekt] watchful and discreet; cautious; prudent.

Colosseum—An ancient amphitheater in Rome, begun AD 70.

Commencement—[*kuh*-mens-*muh* nt] To Begin.

Compulsory—[*kuh* m-puhl-*suh*-ree] Required; mandatory; obligatory.

Conclusive—[*kuh* n-kloo-siv] Serving to settle or decide a question; decisive; convincing.

Condemnation—[kon-dem-ney-sh*uh* n, -d*uh* m-] To pronounce to be guilty, sentence to punishment.

Contemplating—To consider thoroughly.

Contending—To struggle in opposition:

Continent—The mainland, as distinguished from islands or peninsulas.

Conservation—[kon-ser-vey-sh*uh* n] The careful utilization of a natural resource in order to prevent depletion.

Consistent—[*kuh* n-sis-t*uh* nt] Agreeing or accordant; compatible; not self-contradictory.

Conspiracy—[*kuh* n-spir-*uh*-see] A combination of persons for a secret, unlawful or evil purpose.

Cortex—The outer region of an organ or structure, as theouter portion of the kidney.

Covenant—An oath or agreement, deed.

Cumulative—[kyoo-my*uh*-l*uh*-tiv, -ley-tiv] growing in quantity, strength, or effect.

Cymbals—[sim bah l] A concave plate of brass or bronze that produces a sharp, ringing sound when struck.

D

Decay—To decline in excellence, prosperity, health, etc.

Deforestation—The cutting down and removal of all or most of thetrees in a forested area.

Decimated—[des-*uh*-meyt] To destroy or kill a large proportion of: *a plague.*

Deities—A god or goddess.

Delicacy—[del-i-k*uh*-see] something delightful or pleasing, especially a choice considered with regard to its rarity.

Depravity—To make morally bad or evil; vitiate; corrupt.

Deliverance—To set free or release.

Deportation—The lawful expulsion of an undesired alien or otherperson from a state.

Descendants—A person or animal that is descended from aspecific ancestor; an offspring.

Desertification—[dih-zur-t*uh*-fi-key-sh*uh* n] A process by which fertile land turns into barren land or desert.

Detection—To discover or catch (a person) in the performance of some act.

Derived—To trace from a source or origin.

Deuteronomy—[doo-t*uh*-ron-*uh*-mee, dyoo-] The 5th book in the Bible.

Dictatorial—Appropriate to, or characteristic of, a dictator; absolute; unlimited: dictatorial power in wartime.

Differentiate—To form or mark differently from other such things; distinguish.

Diligently—Constant in effort to accomplish something.

Diotrephes—A man mentioned in the Third Epistle of John (verses 9–11). His name means "nourished by Jupiter."

Disciplinary—Training to act in accordance with rules; drill.

Distorted—[dih-stawr-tid] not truly or completely representing the facts or reality; misrepresented; false.

Docetism—[doh-see-tiz-*uh* m, doh-si-tiz] A early Christian doctrine that the sufferings of Christ were apparent and not real and that after the crucifixion He appeared in a spiritual body.

Doctrines—A particular principle, position, or policy taught oradvocated, as of a religion or government.

Drought—A period of dry weather, especially a long one that is injurious to crops.

E

Ecclesiastes—[ih-klee-zee-as-teez] A book of the Bible.

Economy—thrifty management; thoughtful or wise in spending resources.

Elixirs—[ih-lik-ser] A sweetened aromatic solution of alcohol and water serving as a vehicle for medicine.

Elohim—[e-loh-him] God, especially as used in the Hebrew text of the Old Testament.

Emerges—To rise or come forth from or as if from water or other liquid.

Emphasis—Something that is given great stress or importance.

Ensues—To follow in order; come afterward, especially in immediate succession.

Entrepreneur—[ahn-truh-pruh-nur] A person who organizes and manages any enterprise, especially a business.

Epistle—A letter, especially a formal or instructive one.

Exaltation—Raise or elevate, as in rank or character; of high station.

Exclusion—[ik-skloo-zhuh n] To shut or keep out; prevent the entrance of.

Exodus—A going out; a departure or emigration, usually ofa large number of people.

Exile—To expel or banish (a person) from his or her country.

Explicitly—Precisely and clearly expressed, leaving nothing to implication; fully stated.

Exporter—To ship (commodities) to other countries or placesfor sale, exchange, etc.

F

Fending off —To try to prevent something.

Forensic—[fuh-ren-sik] The art or study of argumentation and formal debate.

Forewarned—[fawr-wawrn, foh] To warn in advance.

Francophone—[frang-kuh-fohn] A person who speaks French, especially a native speak.

Frenzied—[fren-zeed] Wildly excited or enthusiastic.

Frontlets—[fruhnt-lit] A decorative band, ribbon, or the like, worn across the forehead.

Futility—[fyoo-til-i-tee] The quality of being futile; ineffectiveness; uselessness.

G

Genealogical—[jee-nee-ol-uh-jee, -al-, jen-ee-] A record or account of the ancestry and descent of a person, family, group, etc.

Gentile—[jen-tahyl] A person who is not Jewish, especially a Christian.

Genres—A class or category of artistic endeavor having a particular form, content, technique, or the like the genre of epic poetry; the genre of symphonic music.

GDP—Gross domestic product.

Gnostic—[nos-tik] Pertaining to knowledge.

H

Hedonism—[heed-n-iz-uh m] the doctrine that pleasure or happiness is the highest good.

Heresy—[her-uh-see] Opinion or doctrine at variance with the orthodox or accepted doctrine, especially of a church or religious system.

Holocaust—[hol-uh-kawst] A great or complete devastation or destruction, especially by fire.

Hymnal—[him-nl] A book of hymns/songs for use in a religious service.

Hypocrites—[hip-uh-krit] A person who pretends to have virtues, moral or religious beliefs, priniciples.

I

Idolatrous—[ahy-dol-uh-truh s] Worshiping idols.

IMF—The International Monetary Fund.

Immense—Vast; huge; very great

Immorality—[im-*uh*-ral-i-tee] Immoral character, or conduct; wickedness; evilness.

Impending—About to happen; imminent.

Importer—To bring in (merchandise, commodities, workers,etc.) from a foreign country for use, sale,processing, reexport, or services.

Imputation—[im-pyoo-tey-sh*uh* n] An attribution, as of fault or crime; accusation.

Indigenous—[in-dij-*uh*-n*uh* s] Originating in and characteristic of a particular region or country; native.

Inevitable—[in-ev-i-t*uh*-b*uh* l] Unable to be avoided, evaded, or escaped; certain; necessary.

Ingredient—[in-gree-dee-*uh* nt]Something that enters as an element into a mixture.

Inhabitants—[nˈhæb ɪ tənt/] A person or animal that inhabits a place, especially as a permanent reside.

Intercessory—[in-ter-ses-*uh*-ree] To act or interpose in behalf of someone in difficulty or trouble, as by pleading or petition.

Intertwined—[ɪn tərˈtwaɪn] To twine together.

Insane—Not sane; not of sound mind; mentally deranged.

Itinerant—[ahy-tin-er-*uh* nt, ih-tin-] A person who travels from place to place, especially for duty or business.

J

Justification—A reason, fact, circumstance, or explanation that justifies or defends.

K

Kaffirs—The word is derived from the Arabic term kafir (meaning 'disbeliever'), which originally had the meaning 'one without religion.

L

Lamentations—[lam-*uh* n-tey-sh*uh* n] The book of the Bible in the OT.

Landlocked—Shut in completely, or almost completely by land.

Latin—An Italic language spoken in ancient Rome.

Langur (the golden)—An Old World monkey found in a small region of western Assam, India and in the neighboring foothills of the Black Mountains of Bhutan.

Legalism—Strict adherence, or the principle of strict adherence, to law or prescription

Leviticus—[lɪˈvɪt ɪ kəs] The third book of the Bible, containing laws relating to the priests and Levites and to the forms of Jewish ceremonial observance.

Licentiousness—[/laɪˈsɛn ʃəs/] Going beyond customary or proper bounds or limits; disregarding rules.

Linguistic—[/lɪŋˈgwɪs tɪk/] Of or belonging to language.

Lyres—[laɪər] A musical instrument of ancient Greece consisting of a sound box made typically from a turtle shell, with two curved arms connected by a yoke from which strings are stretched to the body, used especially to accompany singing and recitation.

M

Mammals—Any animal of the Mammalia, a large class of warm-blooded vertebrates having mammary glands in the female, a thoracic diaphragm, and a four-chambered heart. The class includes the whales, carnivores, rodents, bats.

Manual—Done, operated, worked, etc., by the hand or hands.

Maxims—A principle or rule of conduct.

Metaphor—A figure of speech in which a term or phrase is applied to something to which it is not literally applicable in order to suggest a resemblance.

Meticulous—[mə'tɪk yə ləs] Taking or showing extreme care about minute details; precise; thorough.

Merchant—[mɜr tʃənt] A person who buys and sells commodities for profit; dealer trader.

Microcredit—The lending of very small amounts of money at low interest, especially to a start-up company or self-employed person.

Monarchy—[mon-er-kee] A state or nation in which the supreme power is actually or nominally lodged in a monarch.

Monotonous—[mᴜh-not-n-ᴜh s] Characterizing a sound continuing on one note.

Morality—Conformity to the rules of right conduct; moral or virtuous conduct.

Mozart—Austrian composer (1756–91)

Mundane—Common; ordinary; banal; unimaginative.

Multitude—A great number of people gathered together; crowd.

N

Narrative—[nær ə tɪv] A story or account of events, experiences, or the like, whether true or fictitious.

Nebuchadnezzar—[neb-ᴜh-kᴜh d-nez-er, neb-yoo-] A king of Babylonia.

Nutritional—The act or process of nourishing or of being nourished.

O

Obscured—[ᴜh b-skyoo r] Not clear to the understanding; hard to perceive.

Odor—The property of a substance that activates the sense of smell.

Oracle—[awr-ᴜh-kᴜh l] The agency or medium giving such responses.

Origami—[awr-i-gah-mee] The traditional Japanese art or technique of folding paper into a variety or decorative or representational forms, as of animals or flowers.

P

Pagan—One of a people or community observing a polytheistic religion, as the ancient Romans and Greeks. (No longer in technical use.)

Papyrus—[pᴜh-pahy-rᴜh s] A material on which to write, prepared from thin strips of the pith of this plant laid together, soaked, pressed, and dried, used by the ancient Egyptians, Greeks, and Romans.

Parables—A statement or comment that conveys a meaning indirectly by the use of comparison, analogy, or the like.

Permissive—[per-mis-iv] Habitually or characteristically accepting or tolerant of something, as social behavior orlinguistic usage, that others might disapprove orforbid.

Perplexity—[pər'plɛk sɪ ti] A tangled, involved, or confused condition or situation.

Persistent—[per-sis-tᴜh nt] constantly repeated; continued.

Perspectives—[per-spek-tiv] A technique of depicting volumes and spatial relationships on a flat surface.

Persuaded—[per-sweyd] To prevail on (a person) to do something, as by advising or urging.

Piranhas—Any of several small South American freshwater fishes of the genus Serrasalmus that eat other fish and sometimes plants but occasionally also attack humans and other large animals that enter the water.

Phosphate—[fɒs feɪt] A carbonated drink of water and fruit syrup containing a little phosphoric acid.

Physiologist—[fiz-ee-ol-ᴜh-jist] the branch of biology dealing with the functional and activities of living organisms and their parts including all physical and chemical processes

Plague—An epidemic disease that causes high mortality, pestilence.

Plunge—To cast or thrust forcibly or suddenly into something, as a liquid, a penetrable substance, a place, etc.; immerse; submerge.

Polyglot—Knowing or speaking different languages.

Polytheistic—The doctrine that there is more than one god or many gods.

Populous—[pop-yuh-luh s] Full of residents or inhabitants, as a region; heavily populated.

Principalities—The position or authority of a prince or chief ruler, sovereignty; supreme power.

Predominantly—Having ascendancy, power, authority, or influence over others; preeminent.

Preeminence—Eminent above or before others; superior; surpassing.

Protestant—Any Western Christian who is not an adherent of a Catholic, Anglican, or Eastern Church.

Punitive—[pyoo-ni-tiv] Serving for, concerned with, or inflicting punishment.

R

Radiolucent—[rey-dee-oh-loo-suh nt] almost transparent to electromagnetic radiation, esp X-rays.

Rapture—The carrying of a person to another place or sphere of existence.

Rectangular—Having one or more right angles.

Redemption—Theology. deliverance from sin; salvation.

Remonstrance—[ri-mon-struh ns] To say or plead in protest, objection, or disapproval.

Renaissance—[ren-uh-sahns] The activity, spirit, or time of the great revival of art, literature, and learning in Europe beginning in the 14th century and extending to the 17th century.

Resumption—[ri-zuhmp-shuh n] To go on or continue after interruption.

Revitalizing—[ree-vahyt-l-ahyz] To give new life to.

Riddles—A puzzling question, problem, or matter.

S

Sacredness—Devoted or dedicated to a deity or to some religious purpose; consecrated.

Sane—Having a sound, healthy mind.

Sanskrit—[san-skrit] An Indo European, Indic language, in use since c. 1200 b.c. as the religious and classical literary language of India.

Scrolls—A roll of parchment, paper, copper, or other material, especially one with writing on it: roll of parchment, paper, copper, or other material, especially one with writing on it.

Significant—[sig-nif-i-kuh nt] Important; of consequence.

Smeared—To spread or daub an oily, greasy, viscous, or wet substance on.

Sovereign—[sov-rin, sov-er-in, suhv-] A person who has supreme power or authority.

Sovereignty—The status, dominion, power, or authority of a sovereign.

Species—A class of individuals having some common characteristics or qualities.

Strand—To leave helpless, as without transport or money, etc

Strenuous—[stren-yoo-uh s] Requiring or involving the use of great energy or effort.

Subsequent—[suhb-si-kwuh nt] Occurring or coming later or after.

Successor—A person or thing that follows, esp a person whosucceeds another in an office.

Superlative—The highest kind, quality, or order; surpassing allelse or others; supreme; extreme.

Sushi—A type of food preparation originating in Japan, consisting of cooked vinegared rice combined with other ingredients such as raw seafood, vegetables and sometimes tropical fruits.

Sutures—[soocher] A joining of the lips or edges of a wound or the like by stitching or some similar process.

Sworn—Having taken an oath.

Synagogues—[sin-uh-gog,-gawg] A Jewish house of worship, often having facilities for religious instruction.

Synoptic—[si-nop-tik] Of the 4 Gospels presenting the narrative of Christ's life and ministry.

Synopsis—[si-nop-sis] A brief summary of the plot of a novel, motion picture, play, etc.

T

Theocracy—[thee-ok-ruh-see] A form of government in which God or a deity is recognized as the supreme civil ruler.

Theocratic— [thee-uh-krat-ik] The Rule of God which serves as a supreme law.

Theological—[thee-uh-loj-i-kuh l] Based upon the nature and will of God as revealed to humans.

Transfiguration—[trans-fig-yuh-rey-shuh n] To change so as to glorify or exalt.

Transgression—[trans-gresh-uh n, tranz-] To break or breach of a law, etc; sin or crime.

Treachery—[trech-uh-ree] violation of faith; betrayal of trust.

Truisms—A self-evident, obvious truth.

Tychicus—[tɪtʃíkəs/] Accompanied the Apostle Paul on a part of his missionary journey.

U

UAE—United Arab Emirates, and its capital is Abu Dhabi.

Unheeded—Disregard, ignore.

V

Vindicated—[vin-di-keyt] To clear, as from an accusation, imputation,suspicion, or the like.

W

Wanderings—Moving from place to place without a fixed plan;

Wages—Earnings, emolument, compensation,

Wrought—[rawt] Not rough or crude.

Y

Ylang-ylang—[ee-lahng-ee-lahng] An aromatic tree, Cananga odorata, of the annona family, native to the Philippines, Java, etc, having fragrant, drooping flowers that yield a volatile oil used in perfumery.

Z

Zephaniah—[zef-uh-nahy-uh] A book of the Bible bearing his name.

Zoroastrians—One of the world's oldest monotheistic religions emerged from a common prehistoric Indo-Iranian religious system dating to the early 2nd BC.

References

www.mapsofworld.com

www.gotquestions.org/Book

www.wikipedia.org

www.cia.gov/library/publications/the-world-factbook

www.biblegateway.com

CPSIA information can be obtained
at www.ICGtesting.com
Printed in the USA
BVHW011243180921
616950BV00005B/21

9 781946 174048